CBT TOOLBOX FOR CHILDREN AND ADOLESCENTS

THE COGNITIVE BEHAVIORAL THERAPY MADE SIMPLE FOR MANAGING MOODS AND BEHAVIOURS. COPING SKILLS FOR KIDS AND TEENS TO BOOST SELF-ESTEEM AND FEELING BETTER.

RACHEL DAVIDSON MILLER

CBT WORKBOOK FOR KIDS

CBT WORKBOOK FOR KIDS

STRATEGIES AND EXERCISES TO HELP CHILDREN OVERCOME THEIR EMOTIONAL DISORDERS AND FEARS. THE BEST ACTIVITIES TO HELP KIDS DEAL WITH ANXIETY, STRESS, ANGER, AND ADHD.

RACHEL DAVIDSON MILLER

Introduction

It is challenging to accept or even understand how a young child can feel big emotions like anxiety, stress, depression, and uncontrollable anger. Parents do everything they can to protect their children from situations and events that can cause their child to feel unsafe or unhappy. Despite your best efforts, your child may be secretly suffering and trying to tell you what is going on. The way children communicate these big and distressing emotions is often through inappropriate or harmful behavior.

Children lack a number of skills that can help them work through intense emotions. When these emotions are neglected or ignored, it can lead to serious conditions that can be even more challenging for the child to work through. While parents can do their best to cheer their child up and try to correct unwanted behavior, without understanding the root cause, your child will never overcome what is troubling them.

Cognitive Behavioral Therapy (CBT) is a highly effective form of therapy that is used with children, teens, and adults. This type of therapy establishes specific goals and provides valuable tools and techniques that can help children of any age work through challenging behaviors, thoughts, and emotions.

Unlike many other forms of therapy, CBT focuses on helping patients understand the connections among their thoughts, emotions, and behaviors. By realizing and becoming aware of how each of these elements affects and can impact the other, children can begin to identify what their triggers are.

Parents are an essential component for CBT to be effective. Parents will need to assist the therapy by supporting the practice of the techniques and by teaching their child the skills they may be lacking to help them gain control over their emotions, thoughts, and behaviors. With the encouragement of the parents and the support of a therapist, children can learn to successfully overcome big emotions.

This book will provide you with the information necessary to understand what your child may be struggling with. It will walk you through the process of CBT assessment and goal setting. You will learn how to identify troubling behaviors at home and at school and how you can react to your child when they are struggling. You will find exercises at the end of each chapter to do with your child. There are also additional exercises and tips that you and your child can do together to strengthen their emotional toolbox, increase self-esteem, and set them up for success for the rest of their life.

Chapter 1: What Is Cognitive Behavioral Therapy?

Cognitive Behavioral Therapy is a form of psychotherapy and talk therapy. It focuses on teaching individuals of any age how to deal with their emotions, thoughts, and change behaviors.

What Is CBT for?

CBT is used with children, teens, and adults to show them how to change negative thinking patterns, have a more positive view of themselves and the world around them, and show them how their thoughts, emotions, and behaviors are connected.

Together, the therapist and child, create specific goals that will provide the child with tools to manage their emotions, have more positive thoughts, and control their behaviors.

Who Can CBT Benefit?

CBT can be highly beneficial for many children who struggle with various forms of behavioral issues like impulse control. It can also allow those who may be lagging behind in their learning or developmental abilities. Children who have learning disabilities or challenges will suffer more from low self-esteem, negative thoughts, and emotional control.

CBT can help children cope with the way they are treated by others because of their differences. It allows them to learn skills that will give them confidence and control.

What can CBT help with?

CBT can help children that suffer from:

- Anxiety
- Depression
- Stress
- Anger
- Trauma
- ADHD

Children do not need to have a disorder to take part in CBT. CBT is highly beneficial in showing children at a young age that they can stop, rewire their thinking, and react appropriately to the challenges they face. Your child may be struggling with low self-esteem, social anxiety, emotional regulation, and many other obstacles that are not medically diagnosed. CBT can help you and your child work through these obstacles and will ensure that they have the proper skills to handle more challenging situations as they get older.

Chapter 2: How a Cognitive Behavioral Path Is Structured

Getting your child the help they need may require you to answer a vast number of questions. Though getting your child assessed for CBT can be a little time consuming it is crucial to understand that the information gathered will help you and your child uncover the core problem. Once the problem has been identified, you can establish goals and create an action plan to help your child overcome the problem.

What Are Your Child's Difficulties?

Your child will go through a number of assessments to determine where and what they are specifically struggling with. These assessments are non-intrusive and primarily include a number of different questions that your child, you, teachers, and others involved in your child's life may answer. The question asked will help uncover the problems and address the triggers, history, and additional factors that cause the problem to continue to occur.

Dialogue assessment

An initial assessment will begin with the therapist speaking to you and your child. During this time the therapist will ask a number of questions to uncover the core problem your child may be struggling with. They may use toys or ask them to draw out pictures of some of the things they feel or do. These questions will typically revolve around:

- What the internal thoughts are of the child.
- What behaviors the child exhibits.

- How the child feels about themselves, the people around them, and how they view the world or specific situation.
- When the problem started.
- How intense the problem is when it occurs.

This initial dialogue gives the therapist a general idea if your child is a good candidate for CBT and they will discuss with you the steps of the process.

Testing

Various testing is done to help uncover any underlying conditions your child may have. Testing can focus on:

- Your child's overall health
- Their fine motor skills
- How well they read and write
- The level of learning they possess and if it at the appropriate level for their age (can they count to ten, identify letters of the alphabet, know sight words, etc.)
- Social skills
- Their family dynamic
- Emotional regulation or their level of understanding of emotions

These tests are done in a neutral environment where the child will not feel pressured to perform.

Parent/Caregiver questionnaires

Parents will be given a questionnaire that will give the therapist or team of therapist an overview of concerns you may have. While these questionnaires can be lengthy and cover a range of concerns that address your child's thoughts, emotions, and behaviors, the overall goal is to clearly define what the main concerns are. Assessments for parents will ask you to:

- Identify your concerns, or struggles you are having with your child or notice your child is having.
- Uncover any links between the problem and situation factors. Are there themes, such as rules imposed on the child they are unable to follow or beliefs the child may have that need to be addressed?
- What the links are between your child's emotions, thoughts, or behaviors in a given situation.
- Are there certain people, places, or environmental factors that contribute to the problem?
- What helps resolve the problem?
- What causes the problem to intensify?
- What is the history of the problem? How long has it been occurring?
- When did the behavior start?
- How has the problem progressed since you first noticed it? Has it become more frequent? More intense?
- Is there any history of the problem that predisposed the child, such as family history, troubles in schools? Is there anything that could have triggered the problem to start?
- What causes the problem to persist?
- Who does your child interact with the most? (List family, child care, teachers, peers, and others who are significant people in your child's life.)
- How do the other people in your child's life address the problem?
- What strengths does your child possess?
- What are your family strengths?
- What strengths does your child's school/teachers/childcare offer?
- How motivated is your child to change the problem?
- How much support can the family give in helping change the problem?
- How can your child's school/teachers/child care support in helping change the problem?

- What other support do you have in helping address and change the problem?
- What have you tried in the past to help resolve this problem?
- Why do you and your child think the problem has been unable to resolve in the past?
- What do you and your child think can be helpful in solving this problem now?

You may have more than one concern or problem you would like to have help with solving. You will want to answer each of these questions for each of the problems. Additional question you can expect cover your pregnancy and your child's development.

Teacher questionnaires

If your child attends school, the teacher can fill out a simple questionnaire that will identify issues your child may be having outside the home. Teachers will answer the questions to better assess your child social skills, education achievements, and their ability to follow directions and finish a task. Teacher assessment can also uncover issues your child may be having with transition, understanding material, or learning difficulties and behavioral problems not present in the home setting.

Many questions teachers answer are similar to the ones you will answer as a parent but will focus primarily on the school setting and the skills they already possess. Some of these questions can include:

- Does the child appear happy?
- Does the child play appropriately with peers?
- Does the child have an understanding of material that is appropriate for their age?
- Does the child struggle to sit still?
- Does the child seem to be anxious? If so when is this noticeable?

Often teachers are given specific questionnaires that address what the main problem might be. For instance, if you suspect your child has ADHD, the teacher will be given a questionnaire that is heavily geared towards confirming a diagnosis. If your child has anxiety the questionnaire provided will more focused toward understanding what triggers the anxiety throughout the day.

Once the questionnaire and general assessments have been conducted and reviewed, you will begin to address the core problems that have been uncovered or already discussed. There are often specific areas your child will need help with. The areas your child may need help controlling include:

- Self-defeating thoughts
- Impulse control
- Defiance
- Emotional outbursts or tantrums
- Negative self-talk
- Self-control

Your child may also need help learning new coping mechanisms, problem-solving skills, or how to improve their self-image.

Establishing Goals

CBT is goal-oriented. If your child is approved for CBT, the therapist will work with you and your child to set a specific goal that involves overcoming or changing the problem. When establishing the goal, you will consider:

1. What is the core problem your child is having?

2. How would solving this problem impact your child and the other people involved in your child's life?
3. Can you and your child agree on the goal?

The established goal will be specific and address one problem at a time. This goal will have a measurable time frame, meaning it can be achieved in a realistic and short amount of time. The goal that is agreed upon will be one the child can achieve. Sometimes very short-term goals will be established in order to build your child's confidence so that they learn quickly that they do have the power to change their behavior, thoughts, and/or gain control over their emotions.

Achieving goals

Once a goal has been established, an action plan will be created to move your child forward quickly to achieving this goal. You can help establish goals by following these easy steps:

1. What is the goal?

You want to have a clearly defined goal to begin with. This is a simple step where you ask what it is that you want to achieve. You and your child should agree on the goal set and have an understanding of why this goal is important for the both of you.

2. Where are you starting?

Once you have set a clear goal you want to be honest about where it is your child is starting. What skills does your child have already and what skills do they need to improve? If your child has significant anger issues, than your starting point may include the negative impact their anger has on themselves and others. Look closely at how the problem is affecting the home life, family dynamics, and school. This may not be easy to do and can be disheartening for some parents and the child. But, keep in mind that where you are starting at now is just that: a starting point. Maintain a positive attitude and outlook that it is possible to change where you are starting from. Being honest about where you are starting allows you to clearly see where progress can be made. Looking at things in this manner and reassuring your child that change is possible, encourages them to put in the effort to work towards their goal.

3. What steps need to be taken?

Now that you know where you are starting, you can map out the steps that need to be taken to get your child where they want to go. Each goal you establish will involve taking small steps. Rarely is a goal achieved in just one step. Break down the goals in a way that will make it easily achievable for your child. Think of all the things that will need to be addressed and changed in order for your child to have success. Each step that is achieved will build your child's confidence so though they may be slightly challenged, you still want to ensure that your child is able to accomplish each step.

4. What is the first step you need to take?

Once you have the steps written out you need to put them in order. Think of what needs to be done in order to reach the end goal. Define what the first step to take will be and then ask what the next step needs to be. Some of the most common first steps for your child to take include:

- Learning the different emotions
- Understanding how emotions feel in the body
- Identifying situations where they feel anxious, afraid, sad, or angry

- Understanding how their emotions or behaviors affect others
- Putting themselves in another person's shoes
- Understanding what thoughts are
- Being able to spot negative and positive thoughts

These first steps seem simple, but many children lack the understanding of many of these basic first steps. This lack of basic understanding can often be the root cause of the problem they are having. Once you have established the first step, move on to outline the next step, and so on.

5. What obstacles might stand in your way when you take this first step.

Each step is bound to have certain obstacles that your child will need to learn and overcome. Many times it is our thoughts that stand in the way of making it possible to achieve a certain goal. Maybe your child does not think they are smart enough to learn what they need to learn to achieve the goal. This is an obstacle that will involve supplying your child with positive thoughts that will help them move forward. You will learn more about how to change negative thoughts to positive ones later in this book. For now, simply ask your child what they think may keep them from accomplishing each step. When you have all the potential obstacles laid out, you can learn how to work through them.

6. How will you take the first step?

Now that you have established the goal, outlined action steps, and have considered potential obstacles, it is time to get started. When it comes to getting started, first think about how much time you are going to commit to working on that step each day. Children may not be able to work on action steps for long periods of time but there are many ways you can work on goals throughout the day to get to the end result faster. For instance, if you know your child needs to improve their understanding of basic emotions you can sit down and work on the different emotions with them. You can also incorporate identifying emotions when you read to them, when they are watching their favorite television show, or by talking with them about your day and theirs. You can simply ask them how a character felt when something happened to them, or you can ask them how they think a character feels based on their facial expression and body language. This allows you plenty of opportunities to work toward that first step in a fun and less stressful way.

If you are participating in a CBT session, the therapist will often begin by speaking to your child about the problem and ask for examples and details about when the problem occurs. Then, the therapist will provide tools and address specific areas that are contributing to the problem. These tools will be practiced through role-playing, so you and your child understand how to implement them in daily life. At the end of the session, a homework assignment is typically given to encourage your child to utilize what was covered during the session.

Therapy tools

- **Play** - The therapist will use role-play to help your child understand and use tools to work through a difficult problem. You can do this at home as well. If you know your child had a hard time that day you can ask them to use their toys to replay what occurred. You can then ask them what they could have done differently and how that could have affected the outcome of the situation.

- **Drawing** - Drawing can be utilized to help your child overcome any emotions or behavioral problems. It is also a great way to help them identify negative thoughts. Throughout this book, you will find various exercises that involve drawing to help work through specific problems and to strengthen their skills.

- **Dialog** - How you speak to your child will have a significant impact on their ability to understand and use the tools discussed. Creating a clear path of communication between you and your child is essential for their success. The therapist will go over phrases to use with your child to better encourage and assist them. There is a chapter later in this book that specifically covers how to encourage and open the lines of communication between you and your child.

- **Social Stories** - Social stories can be an effective way to help your child understand challenging topics. Social stories are created to allow your child to identify themselves in specific situations. These stories will place your child as the main character and will describe how they act, think, and the emotions they may be feeling in certain situations. They also address problem-solving techniques and tools your child can use when they are in that situation.

- **Games** - Games are an easy way to teach children basic skills like patience, being a good sport, and problem-solving. You can make time to play any number of games with your child, which will also provide you with one-on-one bonding time. In the last chapter of this book you will find a list of games that are ideal for helping your child identity emotions, practice impulse control, promote communication, and much more. You can easily convert some games you probably have at home into "therapy" games, which you will learn more about later.

CBT utilizes a wide range of simple and effective tools that will help your child reach the desired goal. These tools can be used at home, in school, or in the community. They need to be practiced regularly to ensure that your child can fully understand how and when to use the techniques learned through these tools in everyday situations. The more you practice with your child the more they develop and strengthen these techniques.

The Goal of CBT

Though you will establish a specific goal to work towards, each will focus on the CBT basics discussed in the previous chapter. The tools used through CBT will provide your child with the abilities to:

- Understand negative thoughts
- Recognize emotions
- Make a connection between thoughts, emotions, and behaviors

Each goal established will focus on one of these three aspects:

Evaluating the results:

Once you have begun taking the first steps to reach the goal you will want to evaluate the progress after each step. This will allow you and your child to agree on what may have worked and what still needs to improve. You will also be able to brainstorm different ways to achieve each step. With each step, you should keep track of the tools that were used and how effective they were. You can track your findings in a simply way outlined below.

What are the advantages?

- What tool was used?

- How did this tool help in achieving the goal?

- How often was the tool used by your child in an everyday setting?

- Has this tool helped your child gain a better understanding of their emotions, thoughts, or behaviors?

- What situation did this tool help with?

- How else can this tool be used to assist your child?

What are the disadvantages?

- How difficult was it for your child to use this tool?

- How challenging was it for your child to understand why this tool is beneficial?

- Did this tool make it more challenging for your child to understand or control their thoughts, feelings, or behaviors?

- Why was this tool difficult for your child to use?

- Can this tool be modified to better help your child?

If your child has made a consistent effort to use the tool to help them but did not have success with the tool, then it might not be the right one for them. If your child was inconsistent in using the tool, then you need to address why it was difficult for your child to use this tool and in what situations it was not helpful. From here you can better understand what may help your child more as they move closer to the goals. For example, some children do really well when they have visual cues to remind them how to use the tool, other children need more role-playing, so they become more comfortable knowing when to use the tools. Each child is different and by keeping track of what is and isn't working you will be able to find the right tools the help your child be more successful.

Chapter 3: Anxiety

Anxiety is what helps us avoid dangerous situations and think about our behaviors. It is the natural way we protect ourselves. We often think of anxiety being an adult condition that can affect our daily lives, but it is incredibly common for children to suffer from anxiety as well. For children, anxiety can look like a tantrum, wanting attention, or defiance. Knowing what anxiety is and how it can affect your child will allow you to help your child address and overcome what is making them anxious.

What Is Anxiety?

Anxiety is a natural response when you feel stress. If can cause you to feel afraid of certain situations, people, or things. Feeling anxious about things is a normal and healthy part of development. All children will feel anxious from time to time. It is a normal phase that will come and go as your child grows.

Children may feel anxious when they have seen a scary movie, had a doctor's appointment, are starting their first day of school, or when they are meeting new people. With reassurance and support, most children are able to easily move past their scary feelings and go about their day. Anxiety is often harmless for children to experience.

When a child begins to avoid certain places, people, or things because of their anxiety is when it becomes a problem that needs to be addressed. Even with reassurance and support from their parents, their anxiety can feel overwhelming and frightening to the point where they are unable to confront what is causing them these extreme feelings.

Children can just as easily develop an anxiety disorder as teens and adults can. If left untreated, a child's anxiety disorder can affect many areas of their life such as school, friendships, and participating in fun activities. It can also impact their sleep, diet, mood and behavior. Children who suffer from anxiety disorders are more likely to develop depression.

How to Recognize Anxiety in Children

It can be a challenge to detect anxiety in young children. Children often do not know how to properly express their concerns or may not have the skills yet to even recognize that they are feeling anxious. Their lack of understanding of their emotions may cause them to act out in inappropriate ways or cause them to feel embarrassed about being scared or frightened all the time. Many children try to hide what they are really feeling simply because they don't understand it themselves.

Anxiety can present itself in a number of ways and these signs can often be confused with other conditions like ADHD. Your child may be more restless, hyper, emotional, or withdrawn. Some common anxiety disorders your child may be suffering from include:

1.   Generalized Anxiety Disorder

Generalized anxiety disorder (GAD) occurs when your child excessively worries every day. There is not one specific thing that they become worried about, instead, they worry about a number of things. Some of these things are typical for children such as worrying about taking a test or making friends. But, a child with GAD will worry about these things to an extreme and the worry will be more than just how well they do on a test or if someone will sit next to them during circle time.

Children with GAD worry more deeply, such as if they will disappoint their parents, how smart they appear to others, and if their parents will still love them after making a mistake. These children will also worry about much bigger issues such as if a tornado will occur when it begins to rain or about future events that will occur when they are adults.

When a child is suffering from GAD they struggle to focus and stay on task. They will often seem unhappy and be unable to enjoy fun activities. This constant worry can cause them to become physically sick and interrupt their sleep. Even when reassured that what they are worrying about should not be a concern, the child is unable to stay focused or feel safe.

2. Separation Anxiety Disorder

Most children suffer from a mild form of separation anxiety, especially when they are first left with a babysitter or starting school. After a short period of time, however, many kids will forget that they are away from their parents and will be able to participate in activities and move on in the day. Many children are able to feel safe and secure in their new settings quickly. Children who are unable to feel safe and secure unless their parents are in sight or next to them develop separation anxiety disorder (SAD).

Children with SAD become incredibly anxious when they are away from their parents and this anxiousness doesn't go away over time or as they grow older. It may be difficult for a child with SAD to even be in their own home unless their parent or caregiver is in the same room as them. A child who suffers from SAD may try to avoid situations where they know their parents will not be around. They can also become ill from the anxiety they feel from being away from the parent.

3. Social Anxiety

Social phobia or social anxiety disorder occurs when a child becomes seriously afraid of being around or talking when others are around them. Children suffering from this type of anxiety tend to fear what others may think of them. They are in a constant state of fear of doing something wrong or making a mistake. This causes the child to avoid participating in group activities, answering questions at school, or appearing to be shy when around other people. Many parents mistake their child's social anxiety with them just being shy, and this can cause the child to normalize their behavior which results in it continuing and becoming more extreme. When a child with social anxiety is forced to try to talk in front of others or perform a task, such as being called on in class to answer a question or having attention put on them for being shy, they begin to panic.

Extreme cases of social anxiety can result in selective mutism. In these cases, your child may be so afraid to talk to others they simply do not talk. With selective mutism your child may refuse to talk in school, with their friends, or when out in the community.

4. Phobias

Children can develop specific phobias at a very young age. It is not uncommon for children to be afraid of the dark, loud noises, or certain animals. In many of these instances, an adult can help them feel safe and secure in these situations and the child can calm themselves down and face what they fear. Phobias that become more intense or extreme and last much longer can cause extreme feelings of dread in a child. Children who have specific phobias will do whatever they can think of to avoid confronting what is causing them anxiety. If a child thinks they may confront what they fear they will avoid going to places.

Why Your Child Is Anxious

A child will begin to feel anxious when their body senses any form of danger. Some of the first indication a child may experience when they become anxious is an increase in their heart rate, feeling shaky or jittery, having a hard time catching their breath, or feeling clammy or sweaty. Anxiety can develop because of a number of factors such as:

- Genetics
- Brain chemistry
- Life experiences
- Learned behaviors

One or all of these factors may be causing your child to suffer from anxiety. You can learn to spot specific signs of anxiety at home and in school.

Behaviors at home

Parents may notice some signs of anxiety more easily than others at home.

- Your child may be sleeping less, waking frequently throughout the night or having night terrors or nightmares.
- Their eating habits might change suddenly. Children who are anxious may eat less.
- Mood changes are also common. Your children may become more irritable have an uncontrollable emotional outburst or may get angry in general each day. Your child may cry more or become upset much easier than they used to.
- Children with anxiety may use the restroom more often.
- Your child may have more negative thoughts or constantly be worrying.
- If your child seems to cling to your more often or follow you around wherever you go more than usual, they may be feeling anxious. Children may have a more difficult time going to school, attending birthday parties, or not having a parent or caregiver in sight at all times.
- Anxiety may present itself in the form of feeling physically ill. Your child may complain of stomach aches or headaches.

- Anxious children will often ask "what if" questions that can sound morbid or random.
- Children suffering from anxiety might have fears or worry about future events.
- They can become overly emotional or frustrated when they make a simple mistake.

Behaviors at school

If you are concerned about your child's anxiety, you can ask their teachers if they have noticed any issues. Your child's teacher may be able notice if they possibly have a learning disability that is contributing to the anxiety. Additionally, teachers will be able to inform you if your child may be exhibit any of the following concerns.

- Children may be unable to concentrate or focus as they used to. They may become distracted easily. They will often have a hard time completing seatwork.
- Children with anxiety are often more fidgety. They may appear to be tense or nervous.
- They may not like to participate in group activities like circle time or recess.
- Children may immediately say they cannot do something when given work or ask to complete a task.
- Children with anxiety can have frequent meltdowns.
- They might have difficulty transitioning from one activity to the next.

How to React to an Anxious Child

A child suffering from anxiety can be a challenge. Parents may be trying their best to keep their child calm but can become quickly frustrated by their child's behaviors. Helping your anxious child will also require additional focus on yourself as their parents. It can be exhausting for parents to constantly be supporting and working with their child to help overcome their anxiety and this can lead parents to feel isolated and alone in the daily struggles they are having with their child. Just as you want to do everything to help your child, you also need to give yourself the same love and consideration. Join support groups and talk about any unwanted feelings with a therapist or trusted friend or loved one. The more you feel supported, the better you will be able to help your child.

Be encouraging when your child attempts to face their fears. You do not want to force your child to confront what they are afraid of, as these can be a traumatic experience for the child. Instead, allow your child to take small steps in confronting their fears and let them know you notice their efforts. You can help your child become more comfortable with their anxiety by slowly exposing them to what they are afraid of. This can be done by showing them pictures of what they are afraid of, talking to them about situations that make them anxious, or role-playing situations where they feel anxious.

Talk regularly with your child about how they are feeling. You should reassure your child that you are there to support them and help them feel safe. The more you talk with your child about how they are feeling the more your child will be able to understand what is causing their fear and how they can better cope with these fears.

Exercises

Identify anxiety

Have your child answer and complete the sentences below. You can provide them with examples as listed so they can better understand how they can identify their own emotions in specific situations and the cues their body gives. Then brainstorm activities your child can do to help them feel better when they are experiencing these emotions.

I feel anxious when...

- I have to talk in class
- I met someone new
- I see a big dog
- My parents take me to school
- I have to eat in front of other people
- I am alone

When I am anxious...

- My heart beats faster
- I begin to sweat
- My stomach gets upset or feels like there are butterflies flying around
- I feel shaky
- My head, ears, or body begin to feel hot.
- My palms begin to sweat or feel wet.

When I feel anxious I can...

- Take a deep breath
- Talk to someone about what is bothering me.
- Draw a picture.
- Listen to music.

```
┌─────────────────────────────────────────────────┐
│             I FEEL ANXIOUS WHEN:                  │
│ _____  │
│ _____  │
│ _____  │
│ _____  │
│ _____  │
├─────────────────────────────────────────────────┤
│          WHEN I FEEL ANXIOUS MY BODY:             │
│ _____  │
│ _____  │
│ _____  │
│ _____  │
├─────────────────────────────────────────────────┤
│           WHEN I FEEL ANXIOUS I CAN:              │
│ _____  │
│ _____  │
│ _____  │
│ _____  │
└─────────────────────────────────────────────────┘
```

For parents

Create an anxiety log. This will help you recognize patterns in your child's behavior. You can ask teachers to give you insight and track your child's behavior at school so you can work as a team to better assist your child.

Sample anxiety log

Date:	
Time of day:	
What was happening before you noticed your child became anxious?	
What were the physical, emotional, or behavioral signs you noticed?	
Did anything help calm your child down?	
How long did it take for your child to calm down?	
How intense was your child's anxiety (rate from 1-10)?	
How stressed did your child's anxiety makes you feel (rate from 1-10)?	

Chapter 4: Depression

Feeling sad or in a down mood is normal. It is ok to be disappointed and feel blue from time to time, even for children. Sadness is a core emotion that can be triggered by a number of outside or internal factors. A child may feel sad when they don't get their favorite snack, when a crayon breaks, or when more traumatic life occurrences happens. But, just as with adults or teens, sadness can transition into a more concerning condition if it progresses for long periods of time.

What Is Depression?

Depression is considered a mood disorder that occurs when there are long periods (weeks, months, or even years) of feeling a deep sadness. Children who suffer from this type of mood disorder will be riddled with negative thoughts about themselves, others, or the world around them. They can become overly critical, complain excessively, and only focus on problems instead of trying to find solutions.

Depression is a serious condition that can affect concentration, sleep, appetite, and a child's energy levels. It will also make it more challenging for the child to participate in activities and develop proper social skills. Depression can cause a child to withdraw from their friends and family. Children who are depressed will struggle to complete tasks, will give up when faced with even the smallest of challenges and this only feeds into the disorder.

When a child is depressed their self-esteem can become greatly affected. They will often feel incapable of doing things, feel worthless, and will exaggerate everyday problems. Depression knows no age limits. Many parents think their young child could not possibly be suffering from depression because it is viewed as being an adult disorder. But, depression can affect children in the same way it affects adults but to a higher degree.

Children lack a number of coping skills and the emotional intelligence many adults have developed to navigate through depressive states. This leads to children having a more difficult time expressing what they are feeling appropriately Children will often react with anger or frustration, may pretend to be ill, or may not even be aware of the feelings they are feeling. As a parent, knowing how to spot signs of depression in your young child can help you help them in a more effective way.

How to Recognize Depression in Children

Depression is often overlooked in children for a number of reasons. Often, parents do not recognize the warning signs simply because they think their child is too young to become depressed. Any event that occurs, even if it may not seem like it could traumatize your child, may have a long-lasting impression on them. They may have witnessed someone getting hurt, and although the individual may be perfectly fine, a young child will often misinterpret these events and can become fearful of it happening to their parents or caregivers. This can cause the child to focus on some negative possibility that consumes them causing them to have intense, prolonged periods of sadness.

That said, depression will always have symptoms that you as the parent or caregiver can be aware of.

Why your child is depressed

There are a number of factors that can contribute to childhood depression. Medical conditions such as diabetes or epilepsy, life events, troubles at home, or a family history of depression can cause a child to be more prone to developing depression in their young lives. If the child has suffered from a form of abuse, whether physical or verbal, they are more likely to become depressed. There are symptoms that you can keep a watch for that may give you an indication that your child is suffering from more than just a case of the blues.

Behaviors at home

- Your child may appear to be more on edge or irritable.
- Persistent feelings of being sad or hopeless.
- They may become withdrawn and spend more time alone.
- They are overly sensitive to criticism.
- Change in their sleep, either sleep more often than usual or not enough.
- Change in appetite.
- Having increased temper tantrums.
- They may appear to be more fatigued or have lower energy they usual.
- They may complain of stomach aches or headaches frequently.
- Your child may make comments about feeling worthless or feeling guilty over things that are out of their control.
- They may become more focused on death, or even talk about not wanting to be around anymore.

Behaviors at school

- The child may appear to be lethargic.
- They are unable to focus or concentrate on classwork.
- They withdraw from friends and choose not to participate in group activities.
- They are no longer interested in activities they once enjoyed doing.

- They are quick to anger.
- They feel defeated or are unwilling to try new things.

A child may not show any signs of depression in one setting but will show increased signs in another. For example, a child may appear to be happy and fine at home but at school they may be more anxious and withdrawn. Children can cycle through symptoms where there may be times when they are more temperamental as opposed to withdrawn and vice versa. Though it is unlikely that really young children will attempt physical harm it can occur because they act on impulse. If your child is acting out violently where they pose a threat to themselves or to others around them professional help is necessary.

Depression can be overcome. The child needs to learn to gain control and recognize what is causing them the intense feelings. Parents can show support and love to their child while working with them to develop skills that will improve their lives significantly and these skills will be valuable as they grow older.

How to React to a Depressed Child

If you notice your child may have signs of depression, your first reaction should be to get them the help they need. Getting a diagnosis for depression can be challenging as many of the depression disorders require the child to have symptoms that persist for a year or more. But, even without an official diagnosis, there are ways you can help your child open up about what they are feeling.

Many young children may not understand that they are depressed and therefore resist help or deny that they are feeling so down. Talking with your child is one of the best things you can do to help them. The key to getting your child to open up about what they are feeling is to be present and listen to them when they are talking. You want to show your child that you are there for them to provide them support and love.

Schedule in extra time to connect with your child. Many are unaware of how distracted they are when it comes to spending time with their children. There may be constant interruptions from work or other family members when you are with your child. But dedicating a short amount of time to just play and be with your child, without interruptions, can help them feel less alone and more cared for. Schedule activities that your child likes to do and make time to just relax, laugh, and do something together.

Helping your depressed child will take patience and understanding. Children may act out more aggressively when they are depressed. They may be moodier or more emotional, which can cause parents to become easily frustrated. While it may seem as though your child is purposely being disrespectful or uncooperative, understand that reacting with kindness and love is more effective than reacting with anger and authority. Keep in mind how challenging it is for many adults to navigate this disorder and give yourself and your child some credit as both of you work together to overcome it.

Another key factor to consider is your child's lifestyle. A child that is not getting enough sleep, exercise, or nutritious foods is more likely to suffer from depression. These key factors can also make depression symptoms worse. Be sure your child is eating healthy meals, doing some form of physical activity and getting enough sleep each day. By ensuring these three factors are being met each day, you may notice a significant change in their mood.

CBT is an effective way that many children can learn to overcome their depression and learn skills that will help them avoid falling into this state in the future. Bringing in a specialist to help you and your child is an effective way both of you can learn how to respond to these overwhelming emotions. Not only will CBT work with the child to address the root cause of the depression, but parents will also learn useful tools that they can use to assist their child when they are faced with the challenging situations that can lead to depression.

Exercise

Identifying sadness

With your child, discuss and complete the sentences below. You can provide them with examples as listed so they can better understand how they can identify their own emotions in specific situations and the cues their body gives. Then brainstorm activities your child can do to help them feel better when they are experiencing these emotions.

I feel sad when...

- No one sits with me at lunch.
- My friends do not say "Hi" to me.
- I see someone else get hurt.
- I do something wrong or bad.
- I get in trouble or yelled at.

When I'm sad my body feels...

- Tired
- Weak
- Achy

When I'm sad I can ...

- Ask for a hug
- Talk to someone
- Do something fun
- Laugh
- Tell a joke
- Go for a walk
- Listen to music

I FEEL SAD WHEN:

_____
_____
_____
_____
_____

WHEN I FEEL SAD MY BODY:

_____
_____
_____
_____
_____

WHEN I FEEL SAD I CAN:

_____
_____
_____
_____
_____

Chapter 5: Stress

it can be difficult to understand how a child can suffer from stress. They are supposed to be enjoying their young lives and unaware of the external demands that their parents are stressing over. Children can be highly aware of the stress others are feeling and this can cause them to feel anxious and overwhelmed. Children can also suffer from stress because they are still learning how to properly organize themselves.

What Is Stress?

Stress occurs when we feel overwhelmed or out of control. Our thoughts play a major role in the stress we experience because it is our minds that begin to cause feelings of anxiety and of being overwhelmed. The thoughts we play over in our heads that revolve around certain situations can cause us to feel as though we have no control over what is happening. Stress is a common occurrence when we begin to focus too much on the person we should be as opposed to what we are actually capable of.

For children. this can arise when they feel they have disappointed their parents, when they struggle to understand or learn new things as quickly as others, or when their parents are unable to give them the attention they have been used to. As children grow older they begin to learn to do things for themselves, this is a normal part of healthy development. Some children, however, find these extra responsibilities to be overwhelming when they are applied all at once.

A child may be able to do a great deal for themselves. If the task is broken up and there is plenty of downtime in between one task and another. When these tasks come at them one after another they can quickly lose sight of their capabilities and become overwhelmed by what is expected of them. Parents may not understand why the task is so complex for their child.

41

You may know your child is capable of brushing their teeth, getting dressed and putting on their shoes by themselves. But when you give them all these tasks to do in a set order your child freaks out and all of the sudden doesn't know what to do as though they have never completed the task before on their own.

How to Recognize Stress in Children

Young children have a more difficult time identifying stress and understanding the toll it is taking on their emotions, thoughts, and behaviors. Children who are attending school can feel more stressed as they are learning more challenging things, are trying to make and keep friends, and doing their best to please their teachers and parents. All these elements can lead to a child feeling overwhelmed and unable to control themselves. Children typically act out when they do not know what to do when they are feeling stress as they often have no way of knowing what is causing them to feel the way they feel or how to verbalize what they are feeling.

Why your child is stressed

It is not uncommon for children to suffer from stress. Children who are just beginning school or entering daycare can suffer from separation anxiety which makes them feel overwhelmed and fearful. Additionally, parents who talk about how stressed they are or worried they are about things in their life like finances or health concerns may have a child that takes on these worries themselves. When your child begins discussing or voicing concerns about your job, how bills will be paid, or about a relative or their own health they have most likely overheard these concerns being voiced by the parent. While it is considerate of them to be concerned, what often occurs is that they become stressed about these matters simply because their parents are unknowingly passing these concerns onto them.

Sudden changes in their routine can cause stress. Children thrive on structure. They like to know what to expect and are able to adapt fairly well when they understand how their day is going to run. When this routine is disrupted, children can be overly stressed as they no longer know what to expect. They are not able to go with the flow because they have become used to doing things a certain way for so long. The break in their regular routine can throw off their whole thought process off.

Stress, just as with other concerning mental issues, can be challenging to detect in younger children. They may exhibit mood swings and tantrums that are typical for children. When these short-term behaviors begin to occur more frequently and sporadically this can be a red flag that your child is overly stressed.

Behaviors at home

- Your child may act out more than they typically would.
- They may begin to wet the bed more frequently or unexpectedly.
- They may complain of frequent headaches.
- Your child may have more frequent mood swings.
- Their sleep patterns may change.
- They may begin to suck their thumb or begin other comforting habits such as hair twirling or picking at their nails.
- Your child may overreact to minor mistakes.
- They may become clingier to their parents or caregiver.

Behaviors at school

- A stressed child will be unable to concentrate in the classroom.

43

- They may become defiant and act out randomly when asked to complete a task or follow expected rules.
- They might not complete classwork or turning in homework.
- The child may withdraw from friends or prefer to spend time by themselves.
- They may struggle to participate in group activities.
- Their academic performance may decrease significantly.

How to React to a Stressed Child

If you notice your child may be suffering from stress, the first thing you want to consider and be more mindful of is what and how you talk about the things that are causing you stress. As mentioned, children will quickly pick up on their parents' stress and concerns. Next, you want to ensure that your child is getting enough sleep and eating a healthy diet. When your child is well-rested they are less likely to be irritable and will be able to focus better. When they eat healthy, they will be less likely to feel sluggish or lethargic.

Scheduling in plenty of exercise is also ideal. Physical activity is one of the best ways to reduce stress for both the parent and the child. It also provides an opportunity to spend quality time with your child. This doesn't have to be going for a run or doing sit-ups, simply doing something that your child enjoys doing like dancing around the living room or racing cars bath and forth in a room can be enough. Not only do these play activities get them moving it shows that you are interested in what they want to do.

Talking with your child about what they are feeling can help you understand their behaviors and identify the thoughts that contribute to their stress. When you talk with your child, listen closely to what they are saying and work with your child to come up with some solutions for how they can better manage and react to the thoughts and feelings they are struggling with.

Not all stress is bad. Minor stress helps a child develop properly but they need to learn how to handle the stress in appropriate ways. As a parent, you can model effective ways to manage stress and allow your child to join in when you practice stress-reducing activities. Below you will find a few examples of how to help your child identify what is causing the stress and activities you can do together to reduce stress.

Exercises

Identifying stress

Have your child consider the prompts below. You can provide them with the examples so they can better understand how they can identify their own emotions in specific situations and pick up on the cues their body gives. Then brainstorm activities your child can do to help them feel better when they are experiencing these emotions.

I feel stressed when...

- There is too much noise.
- My parents fight.
- I forget something for school.
- I don't know the answer to something.
- I am asked to do too many things.
- I can't remember what I am supposed to be doing.
- I can't find anything I need.

When I feel stressed by body feels...

- Shaky
- My head hurts
- My body feels tired
- My heart feels like it is racing

When I am stressed I can...

- Ask for help
- Take a deep breath and count to five
- Read a book
- Listen to calming music
- Go for a walk
- Color

I FEEL STRESSED WHEN:

_____
_____
_____
_____

WHEN I FEEL STRESSED MY BODY:

_____
_____
_____
_____

WHEN I FEEL STRESSED I CAN:

_____
_____
_____
_____

Chapter 6: Anger

An angry child can be a serious concern. Their frustration can cause them to act out in harmful and unsafe manners. Children who express their anger in unhealthy ways such as hitting, throwing, harming themselves, or causing harm to others need help in learning suitable ways to express what they are feeling and how to cope with these feelings. Parents who have experienced these extreme, out of control, moments with their child know how scary these moments can be. Taking the time to teach your child and addressing the issues early on will allow them to develop the necessary skills to gain control over themselves and their emotions.

What Is Anger?

Anger is a common emotion we all feel. It can cause us to react immediately to what we feel is unfair, frightening, or stressful. This emotion can come on quickly and in the moment we can temporarily lose control over our impulses.

Anger is especially difficult for a child to manage. They often react intensely to feeling frustrated and this can lead to hitting, biting, throwing objects, screaming and other over-the-top behaviors. Once the feeling has run its course, the child is able to immediately calm down and will be remorseful for the way they acted. What needs to be understood is your child's behavior may be the only way they know how to communicate to you what they are feeling.

Throwing, hitting, screaming, and other dangerous reactions to anger is common for a child that does not know how to express themselves in any other manner. Anger can cause your child to become quickly overwhelmed. They may not yet have the skills necessary to solve the problem they are facing, use their words instead of their body, or control the impulses and intensity when they feel angry.

Many immediately think of this type of behavior as the child simply acting out negatively to get attention or to get what they want. While young children may exhibit this type of behavior to get their needs met it is more likely that they are unable to tell you what they need or want in a more appropriate manner. How you as the parent react to these bouts of frustration from your child can either strengthen the behaviors or allow them to learn more effective ways to handle this extreme emotion.

How to Recognize Anger in Children

Children who suffer from ADHD, anxiety, learning disabilities, sensory processing issues, or autism will have frequent violent outbursts. Each of these diagnoses makes it more challenging for a child to process their emotions and express properly what is troubling them. Not all children have an underlying condition that causes their anger. Many children simply lack the skills or are unable to understand what they are feeling to respond to the situation in a way that is favorable.

Why your child is angry

Children express their anger in uncontrollable ways from lashing out to throwing things or speaking unkindly. When a child is acting out aggressively, they are letting you know they are in a state of distress. They often lack vital skills such as being able to communicate properly, control their impulses or using coping mechanisms or problem-solving abilities. While tantrums are normal for younger children, when they continue past the age of seven and become more intense, this is a red flag that your child is struggling to control their frustrations.

Behaviors at home

- Your child may have extreme, aggressive outbursts regularly.
- Your child may exhibit dangerous behavior when they are angry and may harm themselves or others around them.
- They may experience frequent and long-lasting tantrums.
- The child's behavior may be causing additional stress or strain on the family members.
- Your child may be remorseful and begin to feel negatively about him/herself because they are unable to control their anger.

Behaviors at school

- Teachers may view an aggressive child as out of control.
- The child will struggle to get along with others.
- Classmates may exclude an aggressive child.

How to React to an Angry Child

The best thing you can do when your child is angry is to stay calm. It can be challenging to remain composed and not let your child's behavior affect how you react to their outburst. Keep in mind your kid's behavior may be the only way they know how to communicate their frustration and this often is done in unhealthy and unsafe ways. When you remain calm you are modeling how they can remain calm when they become frustrated. When you respond aggressively to your child's behavior may only reinforce the behavior or give your child the impression that you do not care or are not listening to what they need. They may not be telling you directly what they need but yelling back at your child will not help them solve their problem.

Your child's behavior can be extremely frustrating, especially when they are acting out because they are not getting what they want. It is important that you stay firm in your choices. Caving in and giving your child what they want just to get them to stop the inappropriate behavior only teaches them that this type of behavior will eventually get them what they want. It can be tempting to just give them what they want to make them stop but this will cause the behavior to worsen and the behavior will continue for years.

Give praise to your child when they are able to calm themselves done. You want to encourage your child to react appropriately when they are feeling angry and this will talk a great deal of praise to let them know what exactly they are doing correctly. When your child attempts to express their feelings verbally, tell them they are doing a great job at remaining calm and trying to communicate with you about what is upsetting them. If your child works with you to find a compromise to what has angered them, praise them again. Every effort your child makes to respond to their anger in a mature manner, give them praise for their efforts.

What about time outs?

Time outs can be an effective way to help your child better control and understand there are consequences for their behavior. If your child is under eight years of age, time outs can be a way for them to calm down and then discuss what happened. If your child is over the age of eight, then time outs may not be effective. In these cases, some parents have success with rewards or point system when the child exhibits appropriate behaviors.

Keep in mind, reward systems do not always help a child understand their behavior. When setting up a reward system you want to know what types of behavior you will reward. Some things you can reward include:

- Your child speaks to you with a calm voice even though they are frustrated.
- They take a deep breath when they are getting angry or use another calm technique you have discussed.
- They ask you for help when they are trying to solve a problem.

There are many positive behaviors you can reward but you want to ensure that your child is developing the skills they need to manage their anger. If they are not making efforts to remain in control of themselves aside from seeking out a prize, then a reward system may not be the best option.

Additional suggestions

Notice what triggers your child's anger. Many times situations, activities, settings, or even the clothes they are wearing can be a trigger for meltdowns. When you can identify triggers you will be able to assist your child better in preparing themselves for how to handle what is coming up. So, things you can do to help your child work through their triggers:

1. Establish a routine.

You have probably already heard how much children thrive when there is structure in their day and there is a lot of truth in this. When you establish a routine with your child, they already know what to expect. There is less of a chance that they will become frustrated when it is time to do homework or get ready for bed. Create a routine helps your child feel more confident and safe.

When changes to your schedule do occur, as they will often, be sure that you talk about the upcoming changes in advance with your child. Some kids can easily adjust when they are told something different is going on in their day. Other children may need to be reminded a few days in advance. If you know there will be a change in your child's typical routine, it is best to let your child know ahead of time so they can be prepared.

2. Use timers/give time-based warnings.

If your child gets easily frustrated when it is time to move on to the next activity in the day, giving verbal warnings or setting timers can be a huge help. You want to ensure your child understands that the activity they are currently preoccupied with will need to end soon and another activity will be taking place. When you begin to implement warnings and timers you might need to give a number of them a half-hour prior to the transition. This may seem nagging your child but it helps them prepare for what is coming.

When you use verbal warnings or timers you need to have your child's attention so that you know they understand what will be expected of them. If your child is busy playing with cars or dolls as you are telling them they have 10 minutes left before they have to put the toys away you might get an "Ok," but your child may not have processed what you have said at all. Get down to your child's level and explain to them in simple terms that playtime will be over soon, let them know that you will give them a warning when they have "X" amount of time left, and when the timer goes off it is time to move on to the next activity.

3. Have them repeat what is expected of them.

Many children get distracted easily and do a fantastic job of tuning out what parents and caregivers say to them. This quickly leads to frustration and meltdowns when a child thinks it is unfair that you get to make all the choices. If you have a constant power struggle with your child that triggers an angry outburst it can simply be because your child is not actually processing what you are saying to them and therefore has no idea what is expected of them.

When you are giving warnings, going over consequences, or giving them directions to do something you want to get down to their level and have them repeat back what you have said. Depending on their age you will need to simplify what you are saying or the steps you are giving so they can easily remember what you just said. Do not let them continue with an activity they are currently engaged in if they do not repeat back what you have said. There will be a great deal of resistance when you use these techniques with your child for a number of reasons. You may need to repeat yourself a few times before what you said actually sticks in your child's brain, but staying calm and patient will help your child remain calm and patient.

4. Use pictures or lists.

Younger children may need to have visuals to help them stay on track and to remind them how to stay calm when they are feeling frustrated. You can hang pictures of calming techniques or of what is on the daily schedule so your child knows where to look to know what to do when they are upset and to also know what is coming up next in the day.

Older children can help you create a task list or daily schedule of how the day will unfold. You can create trackers that help them know everything they need to get done in terms of chores, homework, or activities.

Visuals are great in helping children learn how to calm down since they are able to better recall a picture they see over words that are said to them.

Exercises

Identifying anger

Have your child answer and complete the sentence below. You can provide them with the examples as listed so they can better understand how they can identify their own emotions in specific situations and better understand the cues their body gives. Then brainstorm activities your child can do to help them feel better when they are experiencing these emotions.

I feel angry when...

- I get told no.
- Someone else is playing with a toy I want.
- I don't get what I want.
- I make a mistake.
- Someone does not do what I want them too.
- I can't find what I am looking for.
- I hear loud noises.
- My socks aren't on right.

When I feel angry my body:

- Feels hot
- Feels tense
- My stomach hurts
- My head begins to pound
- My heart beats harder
- It is harder to breath

When I am angry I can...

- Take a deep breath
- Walk away from the situation until I am calm
- Color

- Do jumping jacks
- Draw a picture of what made me angry
- Ask for help
- Go somewhere quiet

I FEEL ANGRY WHEN:
WHEN I FEEL ANGRY MY BODY:
WHEN I FEEL ANGRY I CAN:

Drawing

Have your child draw a picture of what their anger looks like. This does not and should not be a picture of themselves, instead, it should be a character that your child creates.

Once your child has created their picture have them give their anger a name. You can now use this drawing your child made to help them identify when their anger is coming out. You can use the name your child gave to the drawing to name their own anger. This helps your child distinguish between their own emotions and responses and those that are occurring because of their anger.

Chapter 7: Trauma

It is not uncommon for children to be exposed to traumatic events. Any form of violence both severe and small can cause a child to feel traumatized. Witnessing a neighbor being taken to the hospital can be traumatic. Seeing a family member become extremely upset or violent can be traumatic for a child. You never want to think of your child as being exposed to traumatic events but it is most likely they already have been. Though it is not unhealthy for a child to experience mild forms of trauma, any type of exposure can lead to serious problems for the child. By understanding what trauma may look and feel like your child you may be able to identify what is causing some of the behavior or emotional issues your child is struggling with.

What Is Trauma?

Trauma occurs when something life-threatening occurs to a person. It can also be the result of physical or personal security being threatened. For a child, this can be anything that causes them to become incredibly fearful or frightened. Children who suffer from trauma feel helpless and unsafe. Children can react strongly to certain situations that can cause them to feel traumatized even if there was no real threat to their life or the life of a loved one.

Traumatic events can include those involving:

- Abuse, either witnessing someone close to them being abused or being abused themselves.
- Domestic violence
- Violence in the community
- Violence in school
- Car accidents

- Illness
- Natural disasters

For a child, experiencing trauma can be incredibly frightening. In many situations, the child is able to be comforted and made to feel safe in a short amount of time. Other children may suffer from a traumatic event that many parents are completely unaware of. Sudden behavioral changes are a clear indication that your child may be suffering from trauma. You may be completely unaware of what could have caused your child to feel traumatized and only by deliberately listening to what your child says and their explanation will you be able to uncover what the true cause is.

How to Recognize Trauma in Children

Many parents dismiss certain events as harmless to their child. But, these events can cause a child to form unrealistic views of the world around them. For example, a child may have witnessed a neighbor being taken away in an ambulance just before they are about to go to school. After school, the child may see this neighbor and know that they are completely fine and nothing is wrong with them. All day at school, however, the child may not only be thinking about the neighbor but may also begin to worry about their parents. They may develop an intense fear that something bad has happened to them while they were at school. Even after the child sees the neighbor is fine, they still may not be able to stop worrying that something may happen to their parents. This simple event can cause the child to be traumatized and they may begin to try to miss out on going to school in order to be sure that nothing has happened to their parents.

As a parent, you may not have even remembered the incident with the neighbor. Only when talking to your child will this detail be revealed. Then you can begin to help your child feel safer and reassure them that them going to school does not mean that their parents are in danger.

Understand the trauma your child is suffering from

Trauma can occur at any age. The younger the child is, the more difficult it is for them to communicate what is causing them to feel so frightened and unsafe. Childhood trauma will typically fall into three categories; acute, chronic, or complex. Understanding the type of trauma your child may be suffering from can help you and your child work through the

1. Acute trauma

Acute trauma occurs after just a single event. This can be witnessing a violent act in the community, car accidents, or the sudden loss of a loved one to name a few. After an acute traumatic event, the child will experience some form of distress that is often short-term. The distress they feel tends to be reflected in their behavior as a way to cope with what they are feeling. With support from loved ones, children who suffer from acute trauma are able to transition easily back into the "normal" behaviors prior to the event.

2. Chronic trauma

This type of trauma is the result of experiencing repeated traumatic events. Children who are exposed to domestic violence or who are or have been abused will develop chronic trauma. Most children do their best to simply ignore or avoid the repeated events, hoping they can just address the issue later or that it will go away. The longer the child tries to ignore this event, the more their negative behaviors will increase and the more likely that they will develop physical manifestations such as chronic headaches or stomach pains.

3. Complex trauma

Complex trauma is the result of continuous exposure to traumatic events. These events are invasive and/or interpersonal such as abuse or neglect. Complex trauma is similar to chronic trauma as it is a repeated event but, complex trauma tends to occur to the child and not just be witnessed by the child. Many times complex trauma is brought on by someone who is supposed to be a trusted caregiver to the child. As a result, the child is unable to form proper attachments with adults or peers. The child will suffer from long term distress making is especially challenging for the child to feel safe and cared for. Other long-term effects can lower the child's self-esteem, and they develop a negative self-image.

Behaviors at home

- Intense emotional outbursts
- Your child may not leave your side or will become anxious if you are out of sight.
- Frequent nightmares
- Trouble falling asleep
- Change in appetite
- Complaints of body aches or pains that have no known cause.
- Your child may appear to be depressed.
- Your child may begin to suck their thumb.
- Becomes fearful of the future
- Children who suffer from trauma may begin to wet the bed.

Behaviors at school

- Children will often show signs of separation anxiety.
- The child will begin to struggle with completing tasks that were never a challenge before.

- The child will struggle to interact with peers.
- Children will have sudden behavioral changes often time disruptive behaviors.
- A child suffering from trauma may not be able to relate to their peers.
- The student may have more difficulty completing schoolwork.
- They may be unable to concentrate.

How to Behave When a Child Has Suffered a Trauma

Your child is feeling a loss of security and be struggling with upsetting thoughts and unpleasant emotions. They need your reassurance that they are safe and this can take constant reminding. Be understanding of their feelings and fears. You don't want to force your child to talk about what occurred unless they are ready and willing to. When they are ready to talk and listen to them and take their concerns seriously.

Limit their exposure to news reports. While you don't want to ignore what happened, you don't want them to have to relive the trauma by hearing news coverage on it. If you do allow your child to watch the news watch with them and talk about what is being reported on.

Reassure your child that it is OK to feel what they are feeling. Do not discredit their emotions or telling them not to feel a certain way. This can lead to your child bottling up big emotions instead of addressing them and working through them. Let your child know how you are feeling too. You may not be feeling the same way but this can let your child learn that everyone reacts differently to certain events. It also helps them recognize that everyone struggles with big emotions, even adults. This can help them feel less alone, embarrassed, or ashamed by what they are feeling.

Schedule in extra one-on-one time with your child. If a traumatic event occurred in your community, then show them that they are still safe and able to have fun doing the things they used to love doing. Show them lots of support and help them talk about their feelings in a way that lets them feel secure and comforted. When a child has suffered through a traumatic event it is important that you remind them they can still have fun. Allow them plenty of time to simply play.

It is important that you maintain regular structure when a traumatic event occurs. Going about your day as you typically would help your child feel more secure. If you are unable to stick to the exact routine you once had, reassure your child that things will return to the way they once were. Do not push your child to do more or give them new responsibilities or chores. Working through trauma can be intense for a child and giving them more to manage can cause extreme behavioral challenges.

Exercises

Identifying worry

Have your child answer and complete the sentences below. You can provide them with the listed examples, so they can better understand how they can identify their own emotions in specific situations and recognize the cues their body gives. Then brainstorm activities your child can do to help them feel better when they are experiencing these emotions.

I feel worried when…

- I am not near my parents.
- I am in an unfamiliar place.
- There are a lot of people near me.
- I have to go to school.
- We drive in the car.

- I hear loud noises.
- I smell smoke.

When I am worried my body feels...

- Shaky
- My head hurts
- My heart begins to be faster
- My palms feel sweaty or cold and clammy
- I may feel weak and tired

When I am worried I can...

- Talk to someone about how I am feeling
- Take a deep breath.
- Ask myself if what I am thinking is true?
- Tell myself that I am safe.

I FEEL WORRIED WHEN:

WHEN I FEEL WORRIED MY BODY:

WHEN I FEEL WORRIED I CAN:

Chapter 8: Attention Deficit Hyperactivity Disorder (ADHD)

Attention deficit hyperactivity disorder (ADHD) is a condition that can impact a child for the rest of their lives. Getting the proper diagnosis and understanding any additional conditions that can be confused and coincide with ADHD is vital for the child to be successful. This condition is more than just behavioral issues, despite what most understand of it. ADHD can negatively impact many areas of a child's life and this in turn will impact their teenage and adult lives.

What Is ADHD?

ADHD makes it more difficult for a child to focus, sit still, and display self-control. This condition is a result of developmental delays in the brain as well as confusion in brain activity. A child with ADHD will struggle at home, in school, and making friends.

Children with ADHD struggle with following directions, even if they are only given instructions with two or three steps. They are unable to stay on task and need constant redirection or reminding. They often miss important details when given a task to complete. Many children can begin a task but never complete it often leading them to be viewed as lazy, forgetful, or defiant.

Hyperactivity is a common symptom of ADHD but a child may display this symptom in varying ways. Some children may literally bounce around the room, run back and forth, or appear to be running on a motor. Others may simply fidget constantly with their fingers, clothing, or kick their feet when sitting. Many children with ADHD who have severe hyperactivity often play rough though they don't mean to.

ADHD causes children to act without thinking. They lack the ability to control their impulses even if they understand the consequences. A child with ADHD simply cannot think that far ahead or stop themselves to fully think about the consequences. Children with ADHD are known to constantly interrupt conversations, grab things without asking, push in line, are unable to wait for their turns, or say things that can be hurtful or rude without realizing it.

ADHD is confusing for children and many will suffer from various conditions as a result. Children with ADHD are more likely to become depressed, anxious, or have low self-esteem. They know that the behavior is unacceptable and even though they try to control themselves they cannot figure out why they are unable to do so. ADHD can look different in every child. Typically a child will be diagnosed with one of three types of ADHD:

1. Inattentive

Children with inattentive ADHD are easily distracted. They are unable to concentrate for long periods of time and have poor organizational skills. The struggles with being able to concentrate results in them missing important details, losing things, and not understanding or able to follow directions. Girls are more likely to be diagnosed with inattentive ADHD over boys. Many assume that those with inattentive ADHD are simply not listening, don't care, or are lazy.

2. Hyperactivity

Hyperactivity ADHD means the child has an excessive amount of energy. This can often be seen as the child not being able to slow down or as many describe it, the child runs on a motor. Children will often talk excessive and fidget a great deal. They will struggle to stay on task because of their need to be constantly moving. Children will constantly interrupt others when talking, be unable to wait their turn, or will act impulsively. They tend to be daredevils because they are unaware of the risk or are unable to think that far ahead to consider the dangers of their behaviors. Those with hyperactive ADHD will struggle to engage in quiet activities and need to constantly play or touch things. Boys are more often diagnosed with hyperactivity ADHD than girls. Many assume those with hyperactive ADHD are just impatient, rude, or simply do not care about consequences.

3. Combination

Combination ADHD means the child exhibits symptoms of both inattentive and hyperactivity ADHD. This is the most commonly diagnosed form of ADHD.

The symptoms your child exhibits will determine the type of ADHD they have. ADHD is a condition that your child can learn to manage but without proper treatment it can affect your child's emotions, behaviors, and can impair their ability to learn things.

Signs of ADHD

Symptoms of ADHD can be linked back to impulsivity, distractibility, hyperactivity, and impulse control. Symptoms will be present in both the home and school setting. Some of the most common signs of ADHD include:

- The child is easily distracted beyond what is considered appropriate for their age.
- The child is hyperactive.
- The child has significant impulse control issues that are not typical for their age.

- The child has exhibit inattentive and hyperactive symptoms from a young age.
- The child does not have health or learning condition that can contribute to the behaviors.

Children with ADHD are more likely to suffer from other emotional or mental conditions. This can make getting an official diagnosis of ADHD challenging. Since ADHD can be present for many years and never be addressed, other conditions can develop over that time period. By the time the behaviors of the child become a serious concern, the other issues may be more prevalent and in turn, may be the first to address. While the other conditions do need to be worked through, not addressing the ADHD can make solving the other problems impossible. If ADHD is not recognized the parent and team working will the child may be focusing on the wrong issues. It is important to know about the other conditions that can contribute to ADHD behaviors.

Common conditions that coincide with ADHD

- *Learning disabilities* - Many children with ADHD suffer from learning disabilities ranging from being unable to read letters correctly or from having really poor handwriting. Children tend to struggle to retain information or remember information and therefore struggle with test-taking.

- *Oppositional Defiant Disorder (ODD)* - This type of disorder results in the child being overly defiant and tending to ignore or challenge anything parents or adults say to them. Children with ADHD will often develop this type of disorder to try to gain control over situations. Since their thoughts and behaviors are viewed as out of control the child seeks out alternative ways to feel in control.

- *Mood disorders* - Children with ADHD have a hard time regulating their emotions. They also suffer from low-esteem which can cause them to develop depression. Because many children with ADHD are constantly being corrected, punished, or negatively viewed because of their behavior. This only adds to the poor view they have of themselves. They can easily become depressed and discouraged because, though they are trying their best to behave, remain in control, and do what is told, they cannot and they do not know why they can't. When others are constantly blaming them for not trying or not caring they feel though it is not worth putting in the effort to change the problems they are having.
- *Anxiety disorders* - Children with anxiety can become anxious and overwhelmed more easily than most other children. Anxiety and ADHD have very similar symptoms making it hard to distinguish between the two. Those with ADHD may become anxious when they have to complete a task or when they are expected to act a certain way and do not believe they are capable of.

Causes of ADHD

Despite what many believe, lack of disciple, screen time, or unstructured home life do not cause a child to develop ADHD. ADHD is the result of development and functional differences in the brain. These neurological differences can be the result of:

- Genes
- Heredity
- Prenatal alcohol or drug exposure
- Environmental toxins
- Head injuries

Though not causes for ADHD, the following can trigger or increase ADHD symptoms.

- Sugar
- Food additives and Preservative
- Too much screen time
- Diets low in omega-3s
- Lack of exercise
- Environmental toxins

Though children with ADHD suffer significantly from behavioral issues these behaviors are often the result of brain development. Cognitive abilities and key competency skills are difficult for children with ADHD to utilize and develop.

Cognitive abilities

ADHD can cause a child to struggle with various cognitive abilities. There are unable to properly sort through, store, and understand a vast majority of new information the obtain throughout the day. This is due to the fact that all the information that passes through their brain is looked at as important. At some point, they are unable to fit more information in their brain and therefore the brain needs to start deleting or removing information to make room for more. The information that is deleted is never examined or properly processed. This is why children with ADHD will often suffer from these common cognitive skills.

- *Concentration* - Children with ADHD are misunderstood in the fact that many think they are unable to concentrate on anything. Children with ADHD are in fact able to concentrate intensely on things that interest them. They can become hyper-focused on specific topics or activities. Children with ADHD tend to struggle

69

with focusing when they are trying to focus on things that seem mundane to them. A child with ADHD needs help learning how to effectively focus their attention on all activities they take part in not just the ones that are of high interest to them.

- **Impulse control** - Impulse control is the ability to stop, think, and maintain control over our desire for something. This can be as simple as waiting your turn to speak in a conversation or not immediately touching things that are in front of you. Children with ADHD have serious impulse control issues because their brains do not allow them to quickly stop before acting out on a thought that runs through their heads.

- **Problem-solving** - Problem-solving is a skill that most children with ADHD lack. They tend to be unable to see things in steps do not fully understand cause and effect. This is why children with ADHD will often act out or have meltdowns when things are not working out the way they want.

- **Metacognition** - Metacognition refers to your child's ability to understand or even be aware of their own thoughts and thought processes. Children with ADHD have thousands of thoughts swarming their heads at any given moment. This is because they have little to no filter in what gets passed on in their brains. most people are able to quickly process and move on from one thought to another. A child with ADHD tends to have multiple thoughts passing through, which they are often unable to determine whether they are important information they should store or information that can be let go.

Competency skills

Competency skills are necessary for everyone to be able to successfully manage their life. A child with ADHD lacks a number of competency skills, which makes completing tasks and following directions nearly impossible for them. These skills are what children need to develop and learn in order to grow and be more independent. The most common competency skills children with ADHD struggle with the most include:

- *Time management* - Time management is a struggle for many children but a child with ADHD has no sense of time. In order to help a child better develop their time management, timers and schedules are essential for a child to learn and understand the importance of time management.

- *Memory* - Children with ADHD have poor short-term or working memory. This is why it is hard for them to complete any tasks that have more than three steps. Many children need to hear directions and rules repeatedly before they begin to stick in the child's memory.

- *Self-regulation* - Self-regulation refers to the emotional control you have. A child with ADHD is quickly frustrated by their emotions, which leads to extreme outbursts. Most children are highly sensitive and feel things more extremely than other children. Though highly sensitive to emotions, many ADHD sufferers are unable to identify their emotions, which causes them to respond in inappropriate ways to them.

How Can Parents Help Their ADHD Child?

The first thing you can do if you suspect your child has ADHD is to have them evaluated by a doctor. The second most important thing to do is to educate yourself. There are a number of misconceptions around ADHD and it can be challenging to understand or be patient with your child as you teach them the necessary skills they need to thrive with this condition. You may become easily frustrated when you have to constantly remind or redirect your child. You may often find yourself saying "why can you just listen?" "how many times do I have to repeat myself?" These statements can be incredibly discouraging to a child with ADHD.

Understand that your child is trying to behave in the most appropriate way but their brains are fighting against them. Children, for the most part, do not actively try to misbehave or disappoint their parents. The strategies and tips list in the last two chapters should be carefully considered and implemented if your child has ADHD. Simple lifestyle changes like eating a proper meal, getting plenty of exercises, and ensuring adequate sleep can help reduce the most common ADHD symptoms.

Chapter 9: Strategies to Increase Self-Esteem

Self-esteem is what encourages us to try new things and bounce back from disappointments. A child's self-esteem should grow as they grow and continue to increase as they develop and explore the world around them. Parents play a key role in a child's self-esteem. Paying attention, giving encouragement, and allowing a child to try something challenging helps a child feel proud and good about themselves. Many factors outside and inside the home can affect a child's self-esteem. Children who lack self-esteem may find it more difficult to control their behaviors. Low self-esteem will also lead to negative self-talk and children can grow into teenagers who make poor choices that can have a severe impact on their life.

What Is Self-Esteem

Self-esteem refers to how you feel about yourself and how you feel about what you are capable of. Having high self-esteem can help you make friends, try new things, and instill a strong, positive belief in yourself. High self-esteem is what allows you to accept and learn from your mistakes. You will be more persistent and able to find solutions to your problems to achieve the goals you set for yourself and throughout your life.

Signs your child is struggling with low self-esteem

A child that has high self-esteem is able to think positively about themselves. They know that they are liked, accepted, and believe in themselves. When a child feels good about themselves they tend to have high self-esteem. Children can suffer from low self-esteem just as teens and adults do.

When a child begins to doubt themselves, they often have a more negative view of themselves. Low self-esteem is a struggle for many children who suffer from behavioral challenges. They begin to focus on how bad they are or the mistakes they have made instead of focusing on the lessons learned or effort they put into doing something. You may notice your child is:

- Self-critical or hard on themselves
- Comparing themselves to others and expressing how they are not as good as their peers
- Only focusing on how often they have failed or messed up
- Not confident.
- Not believing they are able to accomplish things.
- Thinking they will mess up or make mistakes.

A child with low self-esteem will always question what they do and this can lead to them simply avoiding situations and people. They will struggle to make friends as they will think that others will not accept them. Low self-esteem will cause a child to give up before they even try and result in them never reaching their full potential.

Increasing Self-esteem

Self-esteem is important for children because it encourages them to learn and try new things. They develop the skills necessary to feel proud of the things they do and it can help them learn from their mistakes. Self-esteem is what will help your child try again and keep trying when things do not work out the way they originally planned. Just as with any other skills your child may require, you can build self-esteem.

They are many opportunities wherein you can increase your child's self-esteem and provide them with support to increase their self-esteem on their own. Any time your child attempts something new, learns something new, or accomplishes something on their own provides you with a perfect opportunity to give praise and let them know how proud you are of them.

There are many ways you can work with your child to help increase self-esteem from childhood to adulthood. If you notice your child may be suffering from low self-esteem, you can help them raise it so they are more confident in their abilities and like themselves more. The following are some ways you can help boost your child's self-esteem.

1. Seek out learning opportunities.

There are many things your child may need to learn to do on their own. Just as you help them learn to walk, feed themselves, and say the ABC's, there are plenty of new things your child can learn to help them feel more confident. Choose a new task to help your child learn such as:

- Learning to tie their shoes
- Learning to read
- Learning to write
- Learning to ride a bike
- Learning to throw a ball
- Learning to draw
- Learning to braid hair

The list can go on. Choose one task that your child either needs to learn so they can be more independent (like tying shoes), or something they would enjoy learning (like riding a bike). Set aside time each week or day to practice these new activities. This will allow your child to master vital skills as well as give you a chance to encourage and praise their hard work when they achieve the goal.

2. Allow your child to make mistakes

It can be hard to watch your child struggle when they are learning something new. Many parents want to intervene to make things easier for their child and spare them from disappointment or feeling ashamed when they make a mistake. While it is tempting to help your child avoid mistakes, these are valuable learning opportunities for a child.

You will help your child build more confidence in themselves and their capabilities when you allow them to make mistakes. You can teach them new things, show them how to do it, and then let them try for themselves. Whenever they are attempting a new skill it is perfectly fine to offer help to them but after providing them with the help of a few times you should allow them to try on their own.

When you allow your child to try something that challenges them, they can learn from the mistakes they make and feel proud for trying. A child that is able to face their challenges will be more successful as they grow into adults. You can provide your child with opportunities to face new challenges and encourage them to try even if they make a mistake. Again, remind them of how proud you are and how proud they should be of themselves.

3. Give proper praise

Praise can be a key motivation to get a child to do a number of things. Parents praise a child when they have done well in school, have cleaned their rooms, or have done something good. While praising is an effective way to encourage kids to try new things and promote positive behavior, there is a right and a wrong way for praising a child. Some things to keep in mind when you praise your child.

- *Be genuine with your praise.* If you praise your child for doing something good even when you both know it wasn't their best effort, your child will quickly pick up on the insincerity. Find another way to praise them for not giving up or being a good sport. Do not just praise your child to praise them. Find something that will really resonate with them and allow them to feel good about the situation.

- *Focus on the effort they put into what they do.* You will want to avoid giving them praise just because of the end result, such as telling your child how great it is that they got an A. Instead focus on the effort and the skills they needed to get the results like studying hard, practicing a preferred activity like playing an instrument, to improve their skills.

- *You want to praise the progress they are making, the attitude they have as they struggle, and the dedication they exhibit.* This teaches kids to focus on the work they put towards achieving their goals as opposed to associating the end result with whether they were successful or not.

4. Be an example

Your child will automatically mimic what they see you do, so you want to ensure that you are being a good role model for your child or children. When you put effort into everyday tasks, especially those you are not enthusiastic about doing, you teach your child to put effort into the things they may not enjoy doing, but need to get done. Teaching your child to feel proud for accomplishing things like doing their homework, cleaning up after themselves, or even brushing their teeth shows them to take pride in what they do.

Keep in mind that being a good example in these situations requires having the right attitude when you are doing the tasks yourself. If you complain the whole time you are doing the dishes or folding the laundry it is more likely that your child will complain when they have to do something they don't want to do as well. Instead, maintain a positive attitude and model to your child that doing things you do want to do may not be fun but you can be proud of a job well done once you are finished.

5. Develop your child's strengths

One of the easiest ways to help your child increase their self-esteem is to focus on their strengths and the things they enjoy doing. Your child will be more eager to improve on a skill that involves an activity they enjoy and this will allow your child to see what they are capable of. If your child loves to play sports then encourage them to improve on one key aspect of the sport they love, like throwing a football further or leaning to catch a baseball. If your child has an interest in certain topics like horses, race cars, or Legos encourage them to learn more. Take them horseback riding, let the visit an indoor go-kart course, or challenge them to build a Lego city.

When you focus on your child's strengths and interests you not only show them that you are supportive of them but you teach them to pursue things they are passionate about. Allowing them to focus on the things that they enjoy and improve the skills they already possess will help them feel good about themselves.

6. Be patient

When a child hears that they are lazy, not trying hard enough, or is constantly told they can't behave, these harsh words become their internal beliefs. Many parents unknowingly give their children harsh criticism when they are acting out or not listening. This does not motivate or encourage the child to behave differently and often causes the opposite to occur. What your child hears about themselves from others is how they will begin to view themselves and eventually the way they feel about themselves will reflect the negative messages they receive.

Being patient and encouraging to your child when they are struggling or acting out in ways you don't approve of is the best way to help your child. Instead of focusing on what they aren't doing focus on what needs to be done next or what they have already done. This helps your child remain on task and reminds them that they know how to accomplish the task at hand. When your child is struggling significantly show and help them through the obstacles so they know what to do next time.

7. Acts of kindness

Helping others automatically makes you feel good and this is true for your child as well. Though it can be challenging for younger children to fully understand how acts of kindness should make them feel good, teaching them to be compassionate and considerate of others are two key skills for success later in life. When you can, perform random acts of kindness to your kids and allow them to see you doing random acts of kindness for others. This can be as simple as holding the door open for someone at the store or volunteering in the community. Teaching your child that others matter too will help them feel better about themselves when they help another person without expecting something in return. Be sure to praise your child when you notice them doing something kind for someone else, like if they pick up a cup for their sibling or shared their favorite toy.

When your child's self-esteem begins to improve, you will notice that their behavior improves as well. When your child is more confident, they feel more able to control themselves and are able to take more than just themselves into consideration.

Exercises

What are you good at?

1. Think of all the things you CAN do. Do you know how to draw? Ride a bike? Dance? Read? Write? List everything you can think of that you are good at.
2. Of all the things you listed, what is one thing, you want to get better at?
3. Think of different ways you can practice that one thing every day.

Turn your "can't" into "can"!

Trying new things can be scary and hard, at first. The voice inside your head may be telling you something is too hard, or that you *can't* do it. When you hear this voice remind yourself that can try! You can try. If you think something is too hard, remember you can always ask for help.

1. Think of some things that you want to try but have thought was too hard.
2. Who can you ask to help you learn or try this new thing with you?
3. Try the new thing.
4. How did you feel after you tried?

Chapter 10: Communication to Be Adopted With The Child

Communication is the key component to helping your child through any problems they may be having. Whether your child is suffering from anxiety, depression, anger, stress being able to listen and talk with them about what is troubling them is the first step in helping them. Communication involves knowing how to relate and understanding your child by listening to what they have to and by talking with your child to find solutions and help them overcome their problems.

Expressing Empathy

You don't have to agree with your child's behavior or why they feel a certain way, but you do want to reassure your child that you are trying to see things from their point of view. Refrain from focusing on how to fix the issues with your child. Let them know that you are there to listen and work with them through what they are struggling with. Showing your child empathy will and letting them know that you want to understand what occurred or how they are feeling is the first step in helping them identify the problem themselves.

Often times, many children are able to make the necessary adjustments to their thoughts and behaviors just by being able to express and retell their side of the situation. Remain patient and calm as your child walks you through it, and if needed help them identify the flaws in their thought patterns if they do not pick it up themselves.

For instance, if you and your child are playing a game and you win. They may immediately become upset and think they "never win" or that "it's not fair," or they may view themselves as a failure. You can listen to your child express how they are feeling in the situation and they may be able to recognize the negative thoughts and actions that coincide with how they are feeling. From there they may be able to express what they think or feel is simply untrue.

Get Down to Your Child's Level

Effective communication is a combination of speaking to your child with respect and in an age-appropriate manner as well as physically lower yourself to your child's eye-level. When you lower yourself to your child's level they will feel less intimidated and more comfortable talking to you. This also reassures your child that you are listening to what they have to say and you can more easily maintain eye contact with them.

Effective Listening

Communication is not just about how you talk to your child but also how you listen to what your child is saying to you. Throughout this book, listening has been the main component of each of the exercises and problem-solving techniques. This is because when your child feels as though you are really turned into what they are saying they feel more safe and supported. You don't have to agree with what they are saying but you do need to let them know that you hear and understand what they say.

When you listen to your child you want to give them your full attention. Maintain eye contact with your child as they speak. Looking at your phone or away from your child will indicate that you are not fully engaged in what they are saying to you. Just as you would expect your child to stop playing with toys as you are giving them a direction you want to look at your child so they know you are paying attention.

It is not always convenient or easy to stop everything you are doing to give your child your full focus. In moments like these work with your child to find a more appropriate time for the two of you to talk so that you can be completely engaged with them. Reassure them that you understand how important it is that you talk about what they want to talk about and that you want to give them your full attention when you do so.

When you are listening, you need to avoid interrupting your child. It is often difficult to listen without thinking of ways to respond to your child and this can cause you to interrupt them frequently. When you interrupt your child when they are expressing themselves you are indicating that you are not really hearing what they are trying to say. There are ways you can reassure your child that you are hearing them without saying a word. Give them an encouraging smile, head nod, or touch the arm or hand as they speak so they know you are following what they say.

Let your child know that you have heard what they have to say by restating what they have said but using slightly different words. This reassures your child that you have actually been paying attention and you can then begin to work through what is troubling them.

Encourage Your Child to Talk More

It is challenging to get some children to talk about what is going on with them. Many try to avoid these conversations because they themselves cannot make sense of what they are feeling or why they behaved the way they did. There are a number of phrases you can use to get your child to feel more comfortable about talking to you to help them through their problems. Use phrases such as:

- "I'd love to hear more about that."
- "Can you tell me more?"
- "What would you like to talk about?"
- "That sounds interesting, can you tell me more?"
- "Can you explain that to me?"
- "I am listening can you give me some more details about that?"
- "I think I understand, but can you tell me more about what happens when...?"
- "Wow! That is interesting. What happened next?"

Using phrases like these can help open the lines of communication and encourage your child to talk and explain more about what is going on with them. Keep in mind that it takes patience and practice to have effective communication occur between you and your child. Children may only be able to stay engaged in serious conversation for a short amount of time and this can make it frustrating for parents trying to help. Do not try to push your child to talk more than they are ready to talk about. Though you want to help your child, trying to pressure them to open up about their feelings when they are not ready to can cause more behavior problems and make your child feel as though you do not understand what they are experiences.

Chapter 11: Eliminating Negative Thoughts

Negative thoughts can hinder your child's ability to make friends, control behavior, and can have serious effects on your child's self-esteem, mood, and more. Children just like adults need to understand and recognize their negative thought patterns so they can learn to overcome and rewire the way their brain thinks. Changing thought patterns is not something that is quickly or easily done overnight. It takes practice. But, helping your child learn to let go of negative thoughts will allow them to let go of what holds them back. This is a skill that once they learn to master at a young age will never stop benefiting them as they grow up.

Identifying negative thought patterns with your child

1. Blaming themselves

If you notice your child is always blaming themselves for things that have happened, they are struggling with negative thinking. Children who take the blame for things in which they have had no role in the actual outcome have a negative view of themselves. They will often blame themselves for things that are the result of external circumstances which they have no control over such as a family member becoming sick. They will also over-exaggerate the severity of how things turn out even when small mistakes are made like if your child accidental spills their milk and immediately states they are the worst kid in the world.

2. Generalization

Overgeneralization occurs when your child will think the same things will always happen. If they didn't get an A on a test they will immediately think they are stupid or not smart. If they missed kicking a soccer ball, they will immediately think they will always miss and never want to play soccer again. This type of thinking stems from small obstacles that often did not turn out the way they had hoped and then becomes the foundation for their internal belief systems for things that may not even be related.

3. Easily angry

Anger is an instant reaction to a child being overly critical of themselves. If they make a mistake they will get mad at themselves quickly. This anger is their only defense mechanism when they are struggling with something and they are not able to find a solution or have formed the belief that they are unable to find a solution. If your child loses again they will lash out and not want to play anymore. They may often verbally attack the person they are playing with to release some of the negative thoughts running through their head.

4. Unwilling to try new things.

When a child thinks negatively about themselves they will often avoid trying new things. If they do not believe in their abilities to be successful at what they try, they do not bother trying. This is so they do not have to feel ashamed or face additional negative thoughts that will come from them making a mistake or not getting things right on the first try.

5. Always thinking bad things will happen.

If your child constantly looks for the negative in every situation this is a clear red flag that they need help changing their negative thought patterns. Your child will make comments that suggest that they won't have any fun, or that something always goes wrong, or that nothing good ever happens to them. This negative thinking can quickly result in them withdrawing and falling into depression.

Common negative thought patterns in children

1. Black-and-white thinking

With black-and-white thinking your child sees things as all or nothing. They or the situation is either good or bad, or successful or a failure. They look at things in one extreme or another. If something is not exactly the way they wanted, then nothing turned out the way they wanted. For example, if one child in their class didn't let them play at recess, then suddenly none of the kids or no one likes them.

2. Emotional reasoning

With emotional reasoning, your child thinks solely with their emotions and believes these emotions to be facts. A child that lets their emotions dictate their thoughts do so without looking at the whole situation or without trying to reason with how they feel. For example, your child may be afraid of a barking dog and then adopt the thinking pattern that all dogs are dangerous.

3. Overgeneralization

When your child overgeneralizes, they will focus on one small detail of a situation and use this to be their truth for all things related or unrelated to that event. For instance, if your child makes a mistake when they are coloring they will immediately think that they never do anything right.

4. Negative labeling

When your child labels themselves in a negative way they have a difficult time seeing themselves in any other way. Negative labeling is a damaging thought pattern that your child unknowing imposes on themselves and they may not be able to see themselves in any other way. For instance, your child may answer a question wrong while doing homework and jump straight to thinking, "I am so stupid."

5. Minimizing or discounting the positive

If your child is unable to see the positive or constantly discounts the positive facts of a situation they are stuck in a minimizing thought pattern. With this thought pattern you can provide your child with evidence that counters the negative view they have. They will flip this evidence or discredit it so that they still support the negative thoughts. A common example of this thought pattern would be your child tells you that a friend of theirs told them that they loved hanging around them. But, your child adds that this classmate was just saying it to be nice and that they didn't really mean it.

6. Mental filtering

Mental filtering or selective abstraction is when your child only sees the negative in themselves or a situation. They are unable to find the positives. Even if they made one small mistake they will zero in and focus just on that small detail despite any other positive feedback or experience that may have had. For example, your child may have done an exceptional job on their writing assignment but accidently reversed one of their "d's" to look like a "b." This tiny mistake becomes their focus. They don't see how well they did overall just on the small mistake and therefore, all the positive is forgotten.

Keep in mind that a certain level of negative thinking is normal and healthy. When your child has unrealistic thought patterns, however, this can cause serious effects to their emotions and the way they view the world around them. As a result, the way they behave will reflect what they think or they may act out to cope with the negative thoughts.

Explaining Negative Thoughts to Your Child

Negative thoughts can be taught to young children by explaining them using the acronym ANTs (automatic negative thoughts). When teaching young children about negative thoughts you want to help them see these thoughts as ridiculous, not that they themselves are silly for having the thought. You can help your child understand their ANTs by teaching them how to identify their ANTs.

- **A (automatic)** = The thought or phrase just pops in their head. These are uninvited and seem to push their way past everything else you may have been thinking of.
- **N (negative)** = These sudden thoughts are not very helpful or friendly. They may make you feel bad about yourself or about something that happened.
- **T (thoughts)** = These thoughts seem to be talking to you. They sound like you own little voice in your head.

ANTs can be bothersome, but you can use ANTs to explain the thought patterns your child may exhibit when they are in certain situations. You can ask them if the ANTs are bothering them. This will remind your child to stop and look at what is going on in their heads.

Once your child is able to understand and identify their ANTs they can turn them into PETs, positive effect thoughts. To do this explain PETs to your child as:

- **P (positive)** = You can use the thought to help you find solutions. You can reword the thoughts to be encouraging.

- **E (effective)** = The new thoughts should make you feel good about yourself or the situation you are in. These thoughts will help you find the truth or facts in the situation.
- **T (thoughts)** = The inner voice you are hearing is kind and helpful.

PETs are the thoughts your child can carry with them throughout the day and use them to help them through difficult situations.

Changing ANTS into PETs example:

Your child has dropped all their books while getting into the car. Their ANTs may immediately tell them:

- *"I'm such a klutz!"*
- *"I can't do anything right!"*
- *"This whole day is going to be terrible!"*
- *"Why does this always happen to me?"*

If they take a moment to pause and catch their ANTs, they can reframe what they are thinking to create PETs. Their PET thoughts can be:

- *"Well, that was a silly thing to do."*
- *"I made a mess and can ask for help getting everything picked up."*
- *"This is only a small accident, the rest of my day is going to be fun!"*
- *"I tend to drop my stuff a lot. I can find another way to carry my stuff so it is easier for me. I can ask for help to find a better way to carry my things."*

It can take time for your child to think of new and positive ways to look at themselves and the situation they are in. With practice, it will become a natural and effective way for them to overcome obstacles and work through their problems.

It is important that you do not discredit your child's thoughts or refer to them as wrong or right, good, or bad. They are simply things that need to be filtered in and out of your child's brain.

Overcoming negative thinking

Helping your child overcome their negative thoughts first begins with you being honest and taking notice of your own negative thought patterns. It is not uncommon for many parents to unknowingly pass their thought patterns onto their children. The process of identifying your own negative thoughts will benefit you and your child. Do you tend to focus on the stain you have on your shirt and think that everyone is viewing you as a messy slob? Do you tend to think negatively about how you parent just because your child is acting out or because you had to serve up frozen pizza for dinner? Recognizing your own negative thought patterns will allow you to be more understanding how your child is thinking.

Ways you can help yourself and your child overcome negative thought patterns include:

1. Negative thoughts and accurate thoughts.

Find the facts in the situation. When a negative thought does occur, you want to pause and look at the situation in its entirety. Many times negative thoughts are easier to focus on because our brains begin to easily make assumptions about these thoughts. One way you can combat negative thinking is by putting yourself in another person's shoes. For example, your child may jump to the negative assumption that they have no friends or that no one likes them just because someone didn't say "Hi" to them.

You may jump to this assumption if a friend doesn't respond to your text quickly enough.

In both instances, you can look at the situation from a different perspective. The person who did say "Hi" to your child, may not have seen her or had a really terrible morning. Just as your friend may be stuck in a meeting or their phone battery may just be dead.

You can also take the time to remember the facts about a situation. Your child may jump to the negative thought that they are stupid because they got a question wrong on a test. Focus on the facts that other questions were answered correctly.

2. Find solutions.

A lack of problem-solving skills can instantly cause a child to fall into negative thought patterns. Being able to find solutions in situations is a skill that needs to be practiced and overtime results in your child being able to overcome their obstacles with ease and accept when things simply do not work out the way they intend. Going back to the example of your child missing the question on the test. You can review the question with your child and ask them what they may not understand the question. You can also come up with a plan if your child needs to review material before a test.

You can be an example for your child when you come across something that you are struggling with. There are many opportunities that you can include your child in trying to come up with solutions for. You can have your child help you make a schedule for their day so you can get all the important tasks done and have time to spend with them. You can ask your child to help you figure out how to fit all the canned goods in the pantry. Simple tasks that you can easily find a solution for are ideal for getting your child involved so they can develop this vital skill themselves.

It is also important that you remind your child that everyone makes mistakes and this is a part of learning.

Exercises

Create a character

It is important for children to learn and identify their negative thoughts patterns. This will help them look for the facts in the situation instead of focusing on the negativity running through their minds. A fun way you can teach your child to identify their negative thoughts is to create a character.

1. Have your child draw a character that resembles their negative thoughts.
2. Have your child give the character a name. When they begin to show signs of negative thinking you can ask if their character is having an impact on the situation. By labeling the negative thoughts in this way you give your child distance and allow them to look at things from a different perspective (the character's).
3. Once your child has created and named their character you can help your child brainstorm ways to defeat the negative thoughts. Ask your child what they can say to this character when it begins to unleash the negative thoughts

Examples:

- Your child can tell the character that it isn't the boss of them.
- Your child can tell the character that they won't listen to them because they always see things as bad and that maybe they need new glasses.

By teaching your child to identify and come up with strategies to handle their negative thinking. You are not teaching your child to ignore the negative thoughts because that doesn't help them work through or with them. Negative thoughts can be a way to show you how to look at things differently and come up with alternative solutions. Not all negative thoughts are bad as long as you can make them work with you instead of against you. By creating the character with your child you are not dismissing the thoughts, you are showing them how to look at them from the outside instead of just letting them affect them. By brainstorming ways to defeat the thoughts, you are teaching them how they can address these thoughts in a more proactive manner now and in the future.

Affirmations

Affirmations are positive phrases that you say about yourself, to yourself. Creating affirmations is an easy way for your child to not only begin to rethink what they say to themselves, it helps train the brain to think more positively. Some positive affirmations you can teach your child include:

- I am an amazing kid
- I am kind
- I am smart
- I am loved
- I am safe
- I am always helpful
- I am a good problem solver
- I am happy
- I am brave

Chapter 12: Strategies to Manage the Child's Anxiety, Stress, Depression, and Anger

There are a number of lifestyle changes that you can make to ensure that your child is physically and mentally strong. This chapter will provide you with simple ways you can encourage your child to be active, eat healthy, get enough sleep, and practice gratitude. Each of these factors can help them overcome anxiety, stress, depression, and anger.

Get Moving

One of the most effective ways to help your child manage their stress, anger, anxiety, and/or depression is with regular exercise. Exercise helps release the feel-good chemicals in the brain, so you and your child will immediately feel happier once you get yourselves moving. Exercise can also help boost your child's self-esteem and help them feel more mental strength. If your child struggles to get proper sleep incorporating a regular exercise routine can help them regulate their sleep cycle.

Exercise doesn't have to be doing 30 minutes of cardio or running around the block. Below you will find a number of ideas that can make playtime into a regular exercise time as well.

Exercise ideas for kids

1. **Create an obstacle course.**

This is one that can be done inside or outside. You can use household items you already have to create a fun obstacle course that your kids can work through. Some obstacle course ideas can be:

- Setting up a broom that lays across two chairs that your child can crawls under.
- Lining tape on the floor so that your child can jump over each line.
- Setting up small cones or coffee cans that your child can weave in and out of, like doing a soccer or football drill.
- Setting up exercise stations where they have to do 5-10 sit-ups, wall taps (where they jump up and tap the wall as high as they can), or jumping jacks.
- Have a station where they need to run in place for a minute.
- Have them use a spoon to scoop out balls or balloons from one bucket and carry them across the room to put in another bucket.

2. Races

You can set up a simple course for you and your child to race against each other. You can also include some ideas from the obstacle course to make it more fun. if the weather is nice, you and your child can create a hopscotch board and see who can get across and back first.

3. Any sport

You can play a one=on-one match of basketball with your child. You can also simply throw the football or baseball back and forth to one another. You can play tag or have them hit a few baseballs and run around the bases. Soccer is a great sport that you can play with just you and your child. Whatever sport your child is interested in, find a way that the two of you can practice or just play in the front yard together.

4. Dance

Kids love to jump around to music, so whenever they say they are bored turn on some music and let them move around. There are also plenty of videos you can find that will allow your kids to easily learn simple steps to a song and dance along to the music.

5. Go for a walk.

Just getting outside for a quick walk can significantly improve your child's mood. If you have the opportunity to walk somewhere instead of drive take advantage of this time to get your kids outside and get in some quick exercise. If you have a dog be sure to take your kids with you when you take it for a walk or begin making it a routine to walk your dog if you don't already. You can make going on walks into a fun game of follow the leader and is a great way to get some jumping jacks, running, or other jumps in as you go.

Additionally, just allowing your child to play with a hula-hoop, frisbee, jump rope, or on a small trampoline can help them quickly get out energy and it won't feel like exercise.

Yoga

Yoga benefits your child in a number of ways. It allows them to gain control over their body, focus on their breathing, and is a highly effective way to combat anxiety and stress. Yoga can also help teach children body awareness which can help with impulse control and self-regulation.

Yoga sequence for kids

Have your child do each move for 30 seconds. After each move, have them stand up and reach for the stars. Each one has been renamed to imitate an animal making it more kid-friendly and fun!

1. Bear crawl

Have your child get on their hands and knees on the floor. Have them walk like a bear forward and back so that their knees lift off the floor and when their right hand moves up the left leg moves up to meet the left hand. Then alternate so that the left hand takes a step up and the right knee meets the right hand. Have them crawl forward a few steps then back a few steps.

2. Frog

Have your child squat down so their legs are completely bent and their hands can reach in front of them flat on the floor. This should resemble how a frog would sit on a lily pad. You can ask your child to jump up like a frog or they can simply relax in this position for 30 seconds.

3. Cat

Your child will start on the floor on their hands and knees. They should look like a tabletop where their hands are directly below the shoulders and their knees are below the hips. Ask them to arch their back up toward the ceiling as if they were a cat stretching. Then have them lower their back to their starting tabletop position. Repeat this arching of the back for 30 seconds.

4. Cow

You should have your child start in the same position as the cat pose. Instead of rounding their back to the ceiling, they will round down toward the floor and lift their head up towards the ceiling. Then they should round their back, back to their starting position. You can easily combine this pose with the cat pose so that they first round their back up to the ceiling and then immediately round their back to the floor in a smooth movement.

Maintain a Healthy Diet

What your child eats can have a serious impact on their mental health. Children who consume a diet of mostly processed foods, high sugar foods, high-fat foods, or a diet that lacks fruits and vegetables are at higher risk of developing a mental disorder and tend to have more behavioral issues.

Proper diet for kids

Your child's diet should consist of fruits, vegetables, whole grains, healthy fats, and lean proteins. Try to avoid sugary and processed snacks like chips and candy and instead allow them to have fruits, nuts, seeds, or raw vegetables.

You can make their plates more interesting by arranging their food into fun kid-friendly pictures like a butterfly, happy face, or rainbow.

Sleep

Sleep is vital for growing children and unfortunately, children who struggle with behavior issues tends to not be getting enough sleep. When a child does not get enough sleep they are more likely to have mood swings and be unable to concentrate or focus.

Recommended sleep for children

Children under the age of three should get around 12 hours at night. Children between three and 12 should get at least 10 hours of sleep.

To help promote healthy sleep patterns establish a sleep routine with your child. This can include:

- Taking a bath
- Brushing their teeth
- Setting out clothes for the next day
- Reading
- Journaling

You should keep the bedtime routine consistent and make it as calming and quiet as possible. Children should avoid watching television or having any type of screen time for at least an hour prior to bedtime.

Gratitude

Teaching children gratitude from a young age can help reduce their risk of many mental illnesses like depression and anxiety. Gratitude helps your child see all the good things they have in their life and helps them find value in themselves and the world around them. Gratitude can also teach kids empathy and to be more thankful. Starting a gratitude journal is an easy way for children to get into the habit of finding at least one thing to be grateful for each day. This is also a great activity that you and your child can do together at bedtime.

Starting a gratitude journal

Allow your child to pick out a journal that they can use for writing down what they are grateful for. Each night set aside five to ten minutes to write one to three things you are grateful for. You can prompt your child and help them find different things to be grateful for by asking them:

- What was one thing someone did nice for them today?
- What made you happy today?
- What was one thing you did really well today?
- What is your favorite toy?
- Who help you today?

Chapter 13: Exercises to Do Between Parents and Children

It is important for parents and children to work together to overcome the negative thoughts, handle emotions, and adjust behaviors together. When you work with your child through what they are struggling with, many times you will notice that you have been struggling with the same issues as well. The exercises and tools in this chapter are ideal for parent and child to do together. Each of these exercises can help your child develop the skills they need to handle their emotions, combat negative thinking, and control the way they react to overwhelming situations.

Remember to listen to your child when asking questions. It is also important to be honest and open with your child about how you may have struggled or are struggling with some of the challenges they are facing. Always provide your child with the support and love and have patience. Many of these exercises can have an immediate impact on your child's behaviors, others will need to be practiced regularly so your child can learn how to utilize the tools on their own.

Recognizing Emotions

We covered a few ways you can help your child recognize emotions such as asking them how someone feels when watching a TV show or reading a book. You can also have your child draw out the faces of each emotion and have them explain why they drew the face that way for the emotion. Games you have around the house can be used to help your child better understand emotions as well.

Emotions Candy Land

If you have a Candy Land or the Shoots and Ladders board game you can assign an emotion or feelings to each color represented on the board (yellow for happy, red for love, purple for anger, green jealous, orange for grateful) Play as you normally would but each time they land on a color they need to tell a time when they felt that way. You can also have them say what they could have done to make someone else feel that way or have them explain what the feeling is and what activities they can do to help them feel better when they feel a certain way.

Emotions Jenga

You can buy a small Jenga set at most dollar stores instead of using a large version. Color a small circle on each block to represent a specific emotion (red for love, yellow for happy, blue for sad, purple for anger) you can use whatever colors you like and assign each an emotion. Set the game up as you normally would. Each time a block is pulled you or your child needs to tell a time they felt the emotion that corresponds with the color on the block. You can also have your child explain the emotion and ask them what they can do to help them feel better if they get a negative emotion.

Regular Jenga is a great game to help with anxiety. It can help kids become more comfortable with their anxious feelings and remind them that their anxiety is not going to hurt them. The anticipation that builds up waiting for the blocks to fall over is a key factor that can be used to help your child understand anxiety.

Indoor basketball

You can set up a simple basketball hoop using a laundry basket or clean garbage can. Crumble up a few pieces of paper to create the balls. You and your child can take turns trying to get the barber into the basket. If you get the paper in, you get two points. If you miss, you must answer a question.

If you get the question right you get one point. The questions should be written out on index cards and focus on the different emotions. Some sample questions can include:

- What does it mean to feel (happy, sad, angry, worried)?
- If I am (mad, sad, worried), what is one thing I can do to feel better?
- My body feels hot and tense when I am feeling?
- When I am mad I should scream and shout. True or false?
- When I am sad I should talk to someone about what is bothering me? True or False?
- I am smiling and feel relaxed, what emotions am I experiencing?

You can include stories and ask questions about how someone is feeling, what that person can do to feel better, or what the person could have done differently to make themselves feel better.

You can set a goal to reach for how many points you need to acquire before the game is over. For younger children, you might want to say the first person to get to 5 or 10 points wins or for older children 20 points or more.

Breathing techniques

Teaching your child a number of breathing techniques can help them instantly calm their body and thoughts when they are confronting something they fear. These breathing techniques help slow down the heart rate and allow your child to gain control over their emotions. They can be used in any setting and should be practiced frequently, not just when your child is feeling a certain unpleasant emotion.

- Starfish breathing

Have your child stand with their arms stretched out to their sides. Have them take a deep breath as they reach their arms up above their heads. As they exhale, have them bring their arms back down to their sides.

- Blowing bubbles

You can provide your child with actual bubbles to blow or have them pretend to blow bubbles from an imaginary wand. Have them practice taking a deep breath in so that the air fills up their bellies, then have them slowly exhale. If you are using actually bubbles you can tell them that the slower the exhale the breath the bigger their bubble will be. Then have them pop the bubbles as they think about the negative thoughts or emotions they are experienced as a way to release the negativity from their minds.

- Counting

You can have your child inhale for a count of five and then exhale for a count of five. You can also have them hold their hands out in front of them and use their opposite pointer finger to trace the outline of the fingers o. Each time they run their finger up the side of the opposite hand they should inhale, when they run their finger down the side of the finger on the opposite hand they should exhale.

Impulse Control

There are a number of games you can play that will teach your child impulse control without them even knowing. When you are done playing these games you can ask your child how they were able to stop when they needed to or how they were able to follow directions. Then use what they have said to relate to how they can do this in their daily activities.

Red Light, Yellow Light, Green Light.

This is a simple game that can be played indoors or outdoors. You can position yourself at one end of the room or across from your child. When you say green light your child can move forward to try to "tag" you, when you say yellow light your child must slow down, and when you say red light your child must stop. Your child cannot move again until you say green light.

Simon Says

Simon says is a common children's game where one person is Simon and the other must do what "Simon Says" each direct must be started with "Simon Says" (Simon says touch your nose, Simon says hop on one foot, Simon says stop hopping on one foot). If the direction does not start with Simon says, then the child should not do as directed, if they do then the game is over and you can start again.

Freeze Music

This is a fun way to get your child moving and help with impulse control. Play music for your child to dance around to, when the music stops your child must freeze in whatever position they are in. When the music starts again your child can begin to dance again.

Mindfulness

Mindfulness teaches your kids to get in tune with their body, focus on breathing, or become more aware of their surroundings. There are a number of ways you can incorporate mindfulness into your daily lives. Ways to practice mindfulness throughout the day:

- You can teach mindfulness when you go on a walk. As you and your child walk ask them questions about what they feel physically (like the wind blowing on their face), hear, see, and smell. Then ask them how each of these sensations make them feel.
- You can practice mindfulness when you eat with your child by asking them how what they eat tastes and how they think the food helps their body stay healthy and strong.
- You can help your child become more mindful of what they are thinking by asking them what is going on in their heads. Ask them how their thoughts are making them feel. If they are thinking something negative, ask them how they can reword what they are thinking so they feel better.

Journaling

We covered starting a gratitude journal in the previous chapter but journaling to get thoughts and events of the day out of your child's head is a good, general activity to practice. Journaling can help your child work through difficult problems, help them celebrate their victories from the day, and can help them track the progress they are making. You don't have to have a journal set for a specific reason. You can simply ask your child to write about their day, something that interests them, or something that may be bothering them. They can also just write whatever thoughts run through their mind for a set amount of time. If your child struggles to get into the habit of journaling you can have some prompts handy for them to write about.

Journal prompt ideas:

- Who is one person you look up to?
- What would you love to do with your best friend if you knew you would be told No?
- Where is one place you would like to go?
- What was your favorite thing about the weekend?
- What is your favorite subject in school?
- What is a subject you wished you could learn more about in school?
- What is your favorite food?
- Would you rather play a sport or play an instrument? Why?
- What is your favorite season? Why?
- What is your favorite color? How does that color make you feel?
- What is one act of kindness you did for someone else today?
- What is something you want to learn to do?
- What is your favorite cartoon character? If you could spend a day with this character what would you do?

Conclusion

When your child is acting out, they are ultimately trying to tell you that something is hard for them to work through on their own. While you may not want to admit or believe that your sweet child is suffering from intense emotions like depression, anxiety, or trauma, it is not uncommon for children to experience these things. You may have tried everything you could think of to help your child change their behavior without understanding what the root cause was.

This book has provided you with the information that allows you to understand why your child is acting out and what thoughts and emotions they are struggling with. You have to learn how to identify red flags and how you can begin to help your child understand and overcome their struggles.

Throughout this book, you have gained valuable tools and techniques commonly used through Cognitive Behavioral Therapy. You can begin to utilize these tools today to help your child understand how their thoughts, emotions, and behaviors are all connected. You are encouraged to practice the techniques and use the activities on a daily basis so your child can gain the control they desperately want over themselves.

As you assist your child through their struggles, remember to remain calm, patient, and understanding. These big emotions are a struggle for many adults to overcome, just imagine how much your child is struggling. With the information provided in this book, you can help your child overcome the biggest problems and strengthen the skills necessary to be successful in all areas of their life.

References

Angry Kids: Dealing With Explosive Behavior. (n.d.). Retrieved from https://childmind.org/article/angry-kids-dealing-with-explosive-behavior/

Department of Health & Human Services. (2011, December 31). Trauma and children – tips for parents. Retrieved from https://www.betterhealth.vic.gov.au/health/healthyliving/trauma-and-children-tips-for-parents

Dowshen, S. (Ed.). (2015, February). Childhood Stress (for Parents) - Nemours KidsHealth. Retrieved from https://kidshealth.org/en/parents/stress.html

Garey, J., Claire, M., Nyu, New York Times, Los Angeles Times, & American Library Association. (n.d.). How to Change Negative Thinking Patterns. Retrieved from https://childmind.org/article/how-to-change-negative-thinking-patterns/

Khanna, A. (2019, July 24). Want your child to be Active, Fit & Healthy? Retrieved from https://flintobox.com/blog/child-development/exercise-games-kids

Lyness, D. A. (Ed.). (2018, July). Your Child's Self-Esteem (for Parents) - Nemours KidsHealth. Retrieved from https://kidshealth.org/en/parents/self-esteem.html

Lyness, D. A. (Ed.). (2018, October). Anxiety Disorders (for Parents) - Nemours KidsHealth. Retrieved from https://kidshealth.org/en/parents/anxiety-disorders.html?WT.ac=ctg

Matheis, L. (2019, October 4). Signs Of Anxiety In Children: Child Anxiety Symptoms. Retrieved from https://www.anxiety.org/causes-and-symptoms-of-anxiety-in-children

Wright, L. W. (2019, October 16). Signs of Anxiety in Young Kids. Retrieved from https://www.understood.org/en/friends-feelings/managing-feelings/stress-anxiety/signs-your-young-child-might-be-struggling-with-anxiety

CBT WORKBOOK FOR TEENS

THE BEST SKILLS AND ACTIVITIES TO HELP YOU
CONQUER NEGATIVE THINKING AND ANXIETY.
MANAGE YOUR MOODS AND BOOST YOUR SELF-
ESTEEM TO STRESS REDUCTION, SHYNESS, AND
SOCIAL ANXIETY.

RACHEL DAVIDSON MILLER

Introduction

Teens are considered naturally moody, temperamental, and defiant. They want independence but still need to learn how to be responsible enough to handle that independence. For many, the teen years are a struggle. There are many choices they need to make on their own, there is constant pressure to behave and perform a specific way, and they are just beginning to learn who they are and who they want to be. The pressure they feel from others resonates deep within their minds and can paralyze them.

Unfortunately, teens are never directly taught how to handle emotions or how to react appropriately in social settings. While they may be told what not to do, there is often no alternative provided for what they should do instead. Teens are faced with making a number of tough choices throughout their adolescent years. While some breeze through these years, many suffer silently.

The number of teens that hide their anxiety, depression, and insecurity is overwhelming. These years are meant to be the best of their lives. For many, they are a constant battle.

The way they think about themselves during these years is how they will view themselves as adults. The way they cope with their emotions, thoughts, and the behaviors they exhibit in these years will either hinder or propel their success. What many teens lack is the ability to identify and make a connection between their thoughts, emotions, and behaviors.

While they focus on studying, making friends, and attending football games, they neglect to question their thoughts or emotions. They may constantly fight off a negative self-image, limiting belief systems, and intense feelings of fear simply because they don't want to address them or they just don't know how.

Cognitive Behavioral Therapy can provide teens with the knowledge and tools they need to let go of what is holding them back. This type of therapy

addresses the thoughts, behaviors, and emotions that can cau:
act out of control, withdraw from friends, and fall behind in scl
you begin Cognitive Behavioral Therapy, you gain an unders
your negative thoughts, the power they have, and how you can regain
control over them.

What to expect:

This book is designed to introduce you to the practices and techniques
common in Cognitive Behavioral Therapy. You will gain an understanding
of how your thoughts, emotions, and behaviors are all connected and how
they can be causing you to feel anxious, depressed, shy, and lost.
Throughout this book, you will be introduced to key aspects of your life
that you will want to carefully consider and answer questions about. You
will learn how to identify what is truly important to you, the beliefs and
views you have about yourself, and how to overcome negative thoughts
and anxiety.

Each chapter covers a specific topic that will, in the end, allow you to set
clear goals and make necessary changes that will not only affect your
teenage years but will impact your adult life. As you read through the
information, refrain from skipping ahead. Go through each chapter and
answer the questions as they arise.

It is helpful to have a designated journal as you go through each chapter.
This will give you a place to answer questions and more importantly will
give you a place to track your progress. Your journal provides you with a
reference guide that you can turn to remember what you truly want out of
your life.

For Teens

A lot of the information in these pages will benefit you in various ways. Be open and willing to follow through the exercises and keep track of the questions you answer. The material will help you better understand what is causing you to struggle in many areas of your life and will give you the confidence that you can overcome any challenges you face.

For Parents

While this book is geared toward helping teens overcome the struggles they are facing, don't ignore how some of the information in these pages can benefit you as well. Work with your teen to complete the exercise and practice the techniques. Many of the chapters have additional sections specifically for you. You will find tips that can help your child adopt new thoughts and behaviors. You will also find ways to identify when your teen might be struggling and solutions for tackling big emotions and uncomfortable situations.

Use this book to not only encourage your teen to develop the skills that will benefit them throughout their lives but will allow them to grow into confident and successful men and women.

Chapter 1: What Is CBT?

Cognitive Behavioral Therapy was developed in the 1960s by Aaron T. Beck (*History of Cognitive Behavior Therapy*, n.d.). His work focused on treating those with depression when he noticed similarities in the thought patterns these patents had. Not only did he notice patterns in their thoughts, but he also noticed that when these negative thoughts were evaluated by the patient, they were able to adjust their thinking to focus on the truths and facts of the situation. They were able to combat the negative thoughts, which left them feeling more in control and happier about themselves, the people around then, and the way they viewed the world.

What Is Cognitive Behavioral Therapy?

Cognitive Behavioral Therapy is a form of psychotherapy that focuses on how we think, feel, and behave. These three factors shape who we are, the relationships we have, and how we live our lives. Cognitive Behavioral Therapy is a way to help individuals learn to take control of their life and live in alignment with what matters most to them. It has been an effective way to help treat a variety of psychiatric, psychological, physical, and additional health conditions.

Those with a diagnosed medical condition benefit significantly from this form of therapy. The practices, techniques, and tools used in sessions, however, are ones that can help benefit just about anyone who is suffering from negative thoughts, behaviors, and emotions. Adults, teens, and children can use Cognitive Behavioral tools to overcome debilitating anxiety, severe depression, or big emotions they are struggling to make sense of. Teens especially can learn valuable skills that they can carry with them for the rest of their lives. This can aid in the success they have in school, work, and relationships.

Cognitive Behavioral Therapy focuses on learning to stay in the present moment, set goals, and understand how the thought process affects behaviors. Though it is a short-term treatment, it offers long-term positive results. Through this type of therapy, you learn to reprogram your thinking patterns. You also learn the connections that are made between your emotions, thoughts, and behaviors.

Cognitive Behavioral Therapy combines a number of techniques so that the patient can reach their specific goals. Each session includes reviewing progress or concerns. The patient is then given homework that will help them move forward to overcome that negative or dysfunctional thinking. Cognitive Behavioral Therapy is used in varying ways, each focusing on the negative thoughts, behaviors, and emotions that can hold you back.

Types of CBT

- Acceptance and Commitment Therapy (ACT)

Acceptance and Commitment Therapy combines traditional behavior therapy and Cognitive Behavior Therapy in an action-oriented approach to resolve behavioral and psychological issues. This approach involves individuals learning to accept their feelings and thoughts as opposed to avoiding them. Goals are established so that the individual can begin to make the necessary changes and learn how to modify their behaviors so that they can live more fulfilling lives. This type of Cognitive Behavior Therapy is an effective way for individuals to address their fears, reduce stress, and confront their anxieties. The focus is on the way you speak to yourself and view the world around you as a result of a traumatic event or occurrence. You begin to fully understand what is holding you back, why it continues to hold you back, and are taught strategies to overcome and persevere.

- Dialectical Behavior Therapy (BDT)

This type of Cognitive Behavioral Therapy is often used to help individuals with severe mood or personality disorders. Those struggling with forming healthy relationships or who struggle in social settings can greatly benefit from Dialectical Behavior Therapy. The focus of this therapy is providing support to the individual. You learn to focus on your unique strengths to build up self-esteem. You discuss the limiting beliefs, thoughts, and assumptions that run through your mind when in different situations. Specific goals are set to help you identify big emotions you struggle to process appropriately. You learn how to change the way you react to these emotions and how to change your negative thoughts patterns when confronting these emotions so you gain control over them. DBT often combines mindfulness practices with effective thought recognition techniques so that individuals can regulate their emotions and learn new ways to approach distressing or uncomfortable emotions and situations.

- Mindfulness-Based Cognitive Therapy (MBCT)

Mindfulness-Based Cognitive Therapy teaches you how to become more aware of your thoughts. By raising your awareness, you are able to effectively identify negative thoughts and can then learn how to reword and change them to be more empowering and helpful. This type of therapy is one that will provide you with a number of skills and techniques that can be valuable throughout the course of your life.

- Cognitive Processing Therapy (CPT)

Cognitive Processing Therapy is often used to help those suffering from severe mental disorders such as post-traumatic stress disorder. Through this therapy, individuals focus on how they process traumatic events and how they may distort the event. The look closely at the coping skills that have been implemented to deal with the thoughts, behaviors, and emotions when the event is remembered. You learn to identify the inaccurate thoughts that run through your mind and address the unwanted behaviors you exhibit when trying to work through those thoughts when they arise. You learn to evaluate situations to find the truths in them so that you can rewire your thinking and gain control and overcome the events that occurred to you.

Throughout this book, you will be provided with a range of techniques and exercises that are commonly used in many of these types of Cognitive Behaviour Therapy. The most effective strategies for identifying limiting beliefs, negative thoughts, and uncomfortable emotions are explained. You will also be taught how you can begin to solve and eliminate these components that are holding you back. Working through each of the exercises will provide you with the foundation you need to set specific goals that will empower you to reach your full potential.

CBT Principles

The main goal of Cognitive Behavioral Therapy is to help you learn how to resolve the mental blocks, behaviors, and emotions that hold you back. During your teenage years, you will be confronted with unavoidable situations where you will struggle with making the best choices. This can result in unpleasant and big reactions to the choices you make as you either regret the choice or wished you knew how to change the way you react in situations. Cognitive Behavioral Therapy is effective in helping teens overcome limiting behaviors and thoughts because of its core principles.

1. Active Participation

Participants are expected to take an active role in the sessions. They help define goals, create action plans, and practice techniques that will move them forward. Being active involves being aware that work will need to be done to overcome what holds them back. It also involves being open and willing to try suggested exercises and techniques that can help change the way they think, feel, and act. Though some exercises may give immediate results and help them recognize where thoughts are faulty or where behavior needs to be changed, some techniques will need to be practiced. Remaining positive and actively addressing what you want to change will lead you to find great success.

2. Goal-Oriented

When an individual decides to begin Cognitive Behavioral Therapy, there are specific problems that they want to address and resolve. Stating these problems is the first step to managing them. Goals are clear and matched with specific treatment techniques that will allow them to manage and accomplish what they want. Goals should be personal to you, and you need to have a strong desire to achieve them. As mentioned, changing your behaviors and thoughts will take practice and you might not always get it right on the first try. Having a clearly defined goal will keep you committed to the process.

3. Focus on the Present Moment

Cognitive Behavioral Therapy is uniquely different from many other forms of therapy because it focuses on the present moment. The goal is to help individuals recognize their thoughts and emotions and how they impact their behaviors now. There is not much focus placed on what occurred earlier in childhood unless addressing these matters will lead the individual toward their goal. By focusing on what occurs in the here and now, the individual is able to feel more empowered and confident in the ability to control the factors that they face on a daily basis as opposed to dealing with events that occurred in the past.

4. Provide You with the Necessary Tools

Cognitive Behavioral Therapy aims to teach individuals how they can manage their problems by utilizing the skills they already possess. CBT teaches one to strengthen these skill sets and to look at things with a different perspective so that they are able to apply new techniques to situations that have been holding them back. These skills and techniques are valuable tools that individuals can tap into for the rest of their lives to overcome even the most devastating experiences.

5. Relapse Prevention

Individuals are specifically taught and made aware of the key factors that can trigger unwanted experiences like anxiety and depression. By understanding the factors that can contribute to these intense mental blocks, an individual can recognize early signs of the symptoms that can lead to a relapse. When these signs are recognized, the individual can make the necessary adjustments and implement the right tools that will allow them to avoid falling into becoming trapped by their emotions or thoughts.

6. Time-Limited

Cognitive Behavioral Therapy tends to address and successfully help individuals reach their goals in a short amount of time. Some individuals may find themselves able to move past their roadblocks in just a session or two. These shorter treatment plans give individuals more hope and assurance that they will be able to overcome what has been holding them back.

7. Structured

Cognitive Behavioral Therapy provides individuals with a predictable order of steps to take that are necessary for achieving their specific goal in a short amount of time. If you are seeing a therapist, sessions will often begin by addressing the specific problem, going over a tool or technique to help confront the problem, and assigning a homework assignment the individual is to complete before the next session. When they meet again, the session will begin with a review of how the homework assignment went, what changes can be made, and a new homework assignment is given. Sessions are straightforward and organized, which is what makes it such an effective way to help individuals better manage their thoughts, emotions, and behaviors.

8. Addresses Negative Thoughts

Gaining control over one's thoughts is a key focus in Cognitive Behavioral Therapy. Negative thinking can be the root cause of many problems and setbacks individuals are dealing with. Cognitive Behavioral Therapy provides individuals specific ways to identify, reverse, and create new thoughts that are empowering and positive. Addressing the negative thoughts the individual may or may not be aware of is how they will be able to adopt more helpful ways of thinking.

9. Incorporates Various Techniques

Cognitive Behavioral Therapy utilizes a number of techniques in the session and homework assignments. Individuals may learn a list of ways they can help improve their life. This can include meditation, breathing exercises, relaxation training, and exposure therapy, among others. These techniques (which will be discussed in greater detail along with others) are tested by the individual so that they can find the right techniques that are the most beneficial for them.

How Can CBT Benefit You?

The goal of Cognitive Behavioral Therapy is to help you understand your thought process and thought patterns. New patterns are developed by evaluating and assessing past experiences, identifying triggers, and setting goals that will allow you to master your thoughts and live a more fulfilling life.

As a teen, this may sound like a complex process. But, from a young age, we learn to behave in accordance with our thoughts. In this day and age, it has never been more vital for teens to learn how to identify and redirect their negative thinking.

There are many things that Cognitive Behavioral Therapy can help you manage and take control of such as:

- How to identify your negative thoughts.
- How to process big emotions.
- How to manage anger.
- How to process grief or loss.
- How to overcome trauma.
- How to have better sleep.
- How to work through difficult relationships.

The main benefit, however, is recognizing how your thoughts affect your emotions and behavior. It strives to strengthen your ability to identify negative thoughts and re-program your thought process so that you can handle stress, anxiety, fear, and other challenges better.

Cognitive Behavioral Therapy is used to effectively help treat:

- Anxiety
- Attention and focus issues
- Chronic pain
- Depression
- Eating disorders
- Obsessive-compulsive disorders
- Sleep problems
- Trauma

It is used to address the many concerns that involve behavior and the thought process.

Cognitive Behavioral Therapy can help you breakdown challenges into small specific goals. Big emotions like anxiety and depression are organized into more manageable categories (thoughts, emotions, behaviors). and techniques are provided to address each of the categories. By breaking down the problems and issues in this manner, you will be able to specifically target what is the root cause of the problem and create a more appropriate way to deal and manage them.

How CBT Can Improve Areas of Your Life

Teens have to process a number of big emotions and situations. Many of these can be easily faced and many can lead to poor decisions and low self-esteem. Teens who undergo Cognitive Behavioral Therapy often find a solution to their anxiety that surrounds things like test-taking, time management, speaking in class, socializing, and setting goals that will lead to a successful life well after they leave high school. All areas of your life can be impacted by Cognitive Behavioral Therapy.

Relationships

Relationships have a direct impact on the way you think of yourself and the world around you. Feeling connected with others is essential for social development, but having these deep connections can strengthen the image you have of yourself. Relationships are those that you have with your parents, siblings, friends, or significant other. They can also include the relationship you have with coworkers and teachers.

When looking at the relationship area of your life, take note of the following key aspects.

- Which relationships are going well for you?
- What parts of these relationships are working out well?
- Where are you struggling in your relationships?
- How is your communication in these relationships?
- Do you spend enough time with the people in these relationships?
- What is your connection like with these people?

Cognitive Behavioral Therapy can help you recognize how you speak to others and how to boost your self-confidence to build more meaningful relationships. It can walk you through how you feel others view you and how other people's words and actions can affect the way you treat yourself and your behavior. You will learn how to build a clear vision of yourself that will help you feel more comfortable and confident being yourself around others.

Create a list of all the individuals (friends, family, siblings, and others) you have a relationship with. How would you like to improve these relationships? Ask yourself how your thoughts, feelings, or behaviors may be affecting these relationships (good and bad).

School/Work

Some teens are entering or are already in the work field while also attending school. Other teens are focused on school and extracurricular activities. In either case, this is a significant area of life for teens. Since school will be the place you spend much of your young adult life, it is essential that this area of life makes you happy. When you suffer from anxiety, depression, or other stresses, you will feel less ecstatic about this area of your life.

Teens should be taught to find meaning in their school work, extracurricular activities, and the jobs they may have during these years. This will allow them to graduate to pursue careers that give their life more meaning and happiness. Some teens are not challenged enough to become enthusiastic about this area; others feel insecure, anxious, or afraid of their potential (or, in their mind, lack of) to truly excel in this area.

When considering this area of your life, look at:

- What your thoughts on having a quality education are.
- What classes in school do you enjoy most?
- Are there classes you should put more effort into?
- What other activities are you involved in?
- Which of these activities do you enjoy?
- How much do you enjoy your current job?
- What career are you thinking of pursuing after high school?

Spirituality

Spirituality is what makes us feel connected with the world around us. Some people find their spirituality by following a religion, others find it through yoga and meditation, and some find this connection when they are in nature. Spirituality is what gives us more meaning and purpose and reminds us that we are part of something much bigger than just what we see and experience in our daily lives.

When thinking about this area of your life, ask yourself:

- What is important to you?

- What is it that you really care about?
- Are your actions purposeful?
- Do you feel connected to something meaningful?
- What would you like others to say about you?

Health

Living a healthy lifestyle may not be a major concern when you are a teen. Not many are concerned about how all the fast food and chips will impair them in the future. But, poor food choices, lack of exercise, and skipping sleep all impact our mental health as well as physical health. Individuals who commit to a healthy lifestyle are often able to overcome all kinds of difficulties both emotionally and physically. "Healthy" is different for everyone but involves moving your body, eating right, getting enough sleep, and managing stress appropriately.

Questions to ask yourself when thinking about your health:

- How would you consider your overall health?
- Are there any health problems you currently have that affect your life?
- Do you exercise or move your body during the week?
- Do you have any aches or pains when you exercise?
- Does your mood affect your motivation to exercise?
- How would you consider your diet?
- Are your eating habits influenced by your mood or thoughts?
- What is your sleep like?
- Do you find your thoughts keep you awake?
- Are there things that happen in the day that keep you from getting proper sleep?
- What aspects of your health would you like to see improve?

Recreation

While there are many responsibilities teenagers must have, they should also have a number of activities that bring them joy or help them feel recharged. While many teens are involved in a variety of sports or extracurricular activities, many exert themselves in these areas not because it brings them ultimate joy but to please those around them. It is important that the things you spend your time doing are things that you really enjoy. While you may not want to face your parents or teacher's disapproval, taking up hobbies or spending time doing things you want to learn more about or just enjoy are things that will impact your overall happiness. This is an important lesson to learn at a young age. As you get older, you will often find it harder to make time for the things you enjoy; you may find you go off to college just to pursue a future your parents or community expected you to pursue. In the end, you may find yourself pleasing everyone else, but you find that you are not happy or feel like you are not doing what you are meant to do.

When you do not make time for recreational activities you enjoy, you may fall into the habit of doing for others, which results in being unclear about who you are. You will often find yourself sticking to this pattern as you get older. You might ignore the things you truly want to pursue in order to follow what everyone else expects you to. This can result in developing anxiety, depression, and chronic stress.

When thinking about this area of your life, carefully consider and answer the following questions.

- What are some things you enjoy doing?
- Do you feel you have enough time to do the things you enjoy doing?
- Have you noticed that your mood or thoughts have kept you from doing activities you used to enjoy?

Goal Setting

Being able to set and take action to achieve goals is something many teens are never taught to do. You may know how to start and finish projects or homework on time, but you may not know how you can set your own goals or take action to improve the areas of your life you want to improve.

When it comes to goal setting, you want to think about the things that you have wanted to achieve. When have you decided you were going to accomplish something and then took action to work toward accomplishing those things?

Are there times where you may want to achieve a goal but never actually got started?

As a teen, this can work to improve a grade in one of your classes, working to make the varsity team, or finding a job after school. Many teens need an authority figure to motivate or remind them of what they should be doing. If they do not get this external motivation, they are unaware that they have the ability to motivate themselves internally.

Setting goals and taking action on those goals is a skill that will lead you to more success in life. Being able to self-motivate and take initiative on your own to accomplish things will transform you into an adult who is unafraid to face challenges, try new things, or have big dreams. One of the things most teens never understand is that there are so many possibilities in the world, but they get stuck thinking about where they grew up, how they were raised, or the small town that encompasses them is all there is.

Do not be afraid to set goals for yourself. You can begin by setting small goals. You can begin by looking at the areas of your life and identifying where you want to see improvements. Once you have pinpointed the area you want to work on, you can begin to understand what actions you can take to see the changes and reach the goals you set.

Exercise

Consider each of the areas of your life.

Give each area a rating from 1-10, 1 meaning you think this area needs significant improvement and 10 meaning you are completely satisfied with this area and wouldn't change a thing about it.

AREAS OF LIFE	RATING
RELATIONSHIP	
SCHOOL/WORK	
SPIRITUALITY	
HEALT	
RECREATION	
GOAL SETTING	

Chapter 2: Mindset

When faced with a problem, do you tend to think you can find a solution, or do you immediately think the task impossible? Our mindset is what allows us to see opportunities when they arrive. Our mindset can also install a level of defeat that holds us back, makes us fearful, and hinders our ability to be successful throughout our lives. Over time, as our mindset develops fully, it is our mindset that determines the person we become. Your mindset can define who you are. You can let your mindset burden you or your mindset can be the key factor in the shifts you need to make to excel.

What Is Mindset?

Mindset is the way you think about yourself or believe in your qualities, such as your intelligence, physical capabilities, and talents. It impacts how we approach challenges in our lives. Mindset is what allows someone to preserve and be resilient in reaching their goals no matter what complications or obstacles they may face on the way.

For a teen, developing a healthy mindset can affect grades, relationships, and all areas of your life. The right mindset will help you to identify and pursue things you are passionate about. More importantly, the mindset you develop in these teenage years can allow you to succeed after high school.

Having the Right Attitude and Mentality in Life

Developing the right mindset can lead to a life that allows you to truly succeed. When faced with a problem, do you tend to look at it as a way to learn and grow, or do you immediately think it is impossible and that you will be judged or criticized if you are unable to solve the problem correctly? The first mindset allows you to face problems with optimism. It results in your ability to try new things, set goals, and step outside your comfort zone. When we are unable to approach our problems with a mindset of empowerment, we automatically think that a lack of abilities and knowledge makes it impossible to solve or even face challenges.

Fixed Mindset vs. Growth Mindset

There are many categories your mindset can fall into. The two most common are a fixed mindset or a growth mindset. Children tend to naturally have a growth mindset, but as they grow older and face new challenges, this mindset can shift and become fixed. Understanding the components of each and how they affect all areas of your life will allow you to identify where you need to make a shift in your mindset so that you can grow and accomplish the goals you set for yourself.

Fixed Mindset

A fixed mindset can leave us on the defensive. Individuals with a fixed mindset often focus on their failures. They are unable to accept constructive criticism and therefore are unable to make the progress they are capable of to improve their skills and life. Individuals with a fixed mindset tend to think in a black-and-white pattern. They are either smart or intelligent, they are either accepted or rejected, they are either a winner or a failure.

A fixed mindset will result in constantly looking for validation. Children adopt this mindset when they are constantly praised for being or looking smart instead of being praised for their eagerness to learn. As these children become teens, they become fixed on the idea that they will be judged on how smart they are if they do not look or meet the expectations imposed by their parents or teachers. They then fear being a disappointment when they do not live up to those expectations.

They do not focus on the work they put into accomplishing something; they only focus on the end result. Those with a fixed mindset will often have thoughts that focus on:

- Not being able to increase their intelligence.
- Thinking that individuals only have a set amount of intelligence that can not be changed.
- The notion that there is not much that can be done to improve your capabilities or change who you are.
- Believing that the talents you have are the only ones you are capable of. You cannot acquire new talents or skills even if you are presented with an opportunity to learn them

Growth Mindset

A growth mindset is one that motivates you to improve, learn, and work harder for the things you want to accomplish. Those with a growth mindset love to learn new things, welcome challenges, and have an unshakeable desire to learn more. Those with a growth mindset are not afraid to try new things because they are not afraid to fail. Failure to an individual with a growth mindset is an opportunity to learn. New opportunities can come from these failures and a growth mindset allows individuals to seek out these opportunities.

Everything is a learning experience when you have a fixed mindset. Children who are encouraged to explore their surroundings, work through challenging situations, and learn from their experiences, will be more likely to develop a growth mindset. When these children become teens they are able to enjoy the process of learning. They feel a great deal of accomplishment for putting in the work and are not just focused on the end result. They understand that things may not work out the way they intend, but they are able to evaluate what they do, and therefore, are able to learn from mistakes and make the necessary improvements.

Keep in mind that a growth mindset does not mean you think that they can achieve whatever you want just by saying it. Instead, you understand that you must work hard, learn the skills, and educate yourself to be able to reach the goals you set. You understand that if you want to achieve anything, you need to practice and continuously look for ways to improve.

Someone with a growth mindset will have thoughts that include:

- Knowing that they are able to change who they are.
- Knowing that they can learn and increase their intelligence.
- There are many ways in which you can develop your talents and obtain new skills.

Developing a Mindset Capable of Guiding You Toward Your Goals

Developing a growth mindset allows you to set goals and achieve those goals. With a growth mindset, you understand that you are able to live up to your highest potential. This potential, however, is unlimited. There is no ceiling that limits how far you can go. With a growth mindset, you understand that learning and deepening your understanding of the things that interest you will take effort, but that effort is worth the time and energy.

Setting goals is an important step to encouraging a growth mindset. But the focus should not be solely on the end result. Focusing on the process and celebrating the victories along the way is what matters most. Instead of focusing on getting an A in a class, focus on all the new information you are receiving, focus on how this information can benefit you outside the classroom, and focus on the work you are putting in. The end result may not be what you hope for, but it is the steps you take to get the results that matter most. Working hard for something and feeling proud of your efforts is far more important.

Think of your mindset as having its own voice. Your mindset will affect the way you talk to yourself and the more positive your mindset is the more positively you will speak internally to yourself. There are many phrases you might be saying to yourself that undermines what you are actually capable of. Spotting these fixed mindset phrases can help you shift your dialogue to one that is growth-oriented. If you catch yourself focusing on what you are lacking when you face a problem, this is an indication of a fixed mindset. When you notice you are focused on the skills or knowledge that you do not have, you can use this to formulate a plan to acquire the skills or knowledge you do not yet possess.

Switching the way you approach these phrases will encourage you to push yourself and stretch your skills to learn and accomplish what you set out to do. You can challenge these phrases by reframing the dialog you have with yourself. Instead of focusing on not having the skills or knowledge, tell yourself that you can learn and improve on the skills you have that will allow you to accomplish your goals. Instead of worrying about the mistakes you will make or failing at accomplishing your goals, focus on the fact that everyone fails and that if you fail, you will have learned a lot of valuable lessons along the way.

It is one thing to change your internal dialog to move toward a growth mindset, but you can reinforce these thoughts more effectively with actions. For you to truly believe that you are capable of more and growing, you need to take actions that support these thoughts. Practice what you say, set a goal to gather more information by reading more on a specific topic, or set the time aside to practice the skills you want to learn. When you start acting in accordance with your thoughts, your mindset will continue to grow and encourage you to do more.

Exercises

Face Your Fears

What is one thing that you have been wanting to do but fear has been holding you back?

_____

_____

_____

_____

_____

_____

Consider what is the worst thing that can happen?

_____

_____

_____

_____

_____

_____

How likely is it that this outcome will occur?

_____

_____

_____

_____

_____

_____

If this outcome were to occur, how would that really affect the person you are?

_____

_____

_____

_____

_____

_____

Now think of the opposite outcome.

_____

_____

_____

_____

_____

_____

What steps can you take to better ensure this outcome would occur?

_____

_____

_____

_____

_____

_____

Consider things you could do that would be outside of your comfort zone.

_____

_____

_____

_____

_____

_____

Exposure

When it comes to shifting your mindset, one of the things you can do to have a growth mindset is to gradually expose yourself to the things you want to do but let fear or anxiety hold you back.

Consider situations where you tend to have a more negative or fixed mindset.

What situation do you avoid because of a fixed mindset of not believing in yourself or your abilities?

_____

_____

_____

_____

_____

_____

How can you face the fears you have about these situations?

_____

_____

_____

_____

_____

_____

Create a list of small steps you can take that will allow you to feel more comfortable and confident in these settings.

1. _____

2. _____

3. _____

4. _____

5. _____

Choose one thing from this list and actually follow through and do it.

Chapter 3: Beliefs

Beliefs begin to develop at a young age. We often do not recognize the negative or positive beliefs we hold until much later in life. These beliefs will have a major impact on all areas of your life and will affect the way you approach the people you encounter and the situations you face.

What Are Beliefs?

Beliefs are the core assumptions or thoughts you form about yourself and the world around you. These inner beliefs tend to playback over and over throughout the course of your life. We take these beliefs as facts and assume they are true without really questioning where they manifest from or what has contributed to their formation. They will affect the way you view the world around you. You can either develop a belief system that helps you feel empowered, confident, and capable, or you can develop a set of beliefs that makes you cynical, defeated, and made to feel unimportant.

What one must understand is that these beliefs do not have to be fixed in place. Our core beliefs can be completely wrong, and we can change them! Some examples of untrue beliefs:

- Everyone is better than me.
- I'm stupid.
- Everyone is so selfish.
- Everyone takes advantage of me.

These beliefs may be deeply ingrained in our everyday life. The way we act, think, and how we feel is affected by these core beliefs. Your core beliefs can be wrong, and they can be changed. Core beliefs can result in a deeply rooted need to do things perfectly and receive the approval from those around us. As a teen, these two components can result in negative beliefs that will impact you throughout your life.

Perfectionism

This negative belief forms when you feel as though you are not good enough. This type of belief can push you to better areas of your life. While wanting to improve upon things in your life is a great attribute to have, perfectionism can result in constant let downs and failures. Perfectionism can make you feel as though you are less than those around you, unworthy, or unable to accomplish what you desire.

The way you talk to yourself can help you identify if you have perfectionist beliefs. Constantly making should comments like, "I should do better in school," "I should have tried harder during practice," and "I should have said something different during class" show a perfectionist mindset. These should statement you say to yourself will make you feel as though others do not accept you or that you are not trying your best to reach your full potential.

Having a belief system of perfectionism can result in feeling alone, panic attacks, anxiety, and depression. This makes it difficult to set and move toward the goals you want to reach. Those with a perfectionist belief system will often never feel satisfied with themselves or feel that others will never accept them for who they are. You will find yourself placing more merit on your accomplishments than on your values, and therefore, your self-worth can be greatly hindered.

Need for Approval

As a teen, you want to be liked by your peers and exceed the expectations your teachers or parents have placed on you. It is normal to want to be liked and included, but the constant need for approval can lead to low self-esteem, anxiety, anger, and disappointment. When you begin to measure your self-worth by how much others like you, you will begin to develop an overly critical inner dialog with yourself. You will jump to assumptions and run through list after list of all the things you should have said, could have done, and what ifs. This constant need for approval from others can leave you on the defensive and can, as a result, begin to push people away from you.

Not everyone is going to like you and be your friend, and most of the time, this is going to be for absolutely no reason. There is nothing wrong with that, and there is nothing wrong with the person you are. But this belief system of needing the approval of others will cause you to lose your own self-identity. You will constantly be doing things or acting a certain way because you think it is how you will get more approval from others.

How Your Beliefs Affect the Way You Think and Act

Your beliefs will affect your behavior in every situation. The way you behave will reinforce your beliefs. When we have negative beliefs about ourselves, we will feel inadequate, undeserving, and simply terrible. When we create a belief about ourselves, we often automatically take it as truth in any situation. Our beliefs are how we identify things and people as being either good or bad, whether a situation is dangerous or safe, or if our behavior is acceptable or unacceptable. They play an integral part in whether we believe our goals are achievable or not.

We can also project our core beliefs onto others. This projection is based on how we assume others view us. If you are bullied, you might begin to form the belief around what the bully says to you and begin to perceive yourself in this same way. Eventually, you will begin to think that everyone you meet will perceive in this way as well.

143

Beliefs are deeply rooted in all areas of our lives. We may have hundreds of beliefs that dictate our behavior, thoughts, and emotions. Our beliefs will result in having automatic thoughts about ourselves and those around us. Some of these thoughts serve us well, but many are not based on facts and can hold us back. Beliefs are connected to our subconscious mind, which is constantly looking to validate these beliefs. When we have negative or limiting beliefs, we unknowingly behave and think in a way that will further support these beliefs.

When you have negative beliefs, you ignore any evidence that opposes these beliefs and instead focus on the things that strengthen them. Our beliefs act as filters. We see what reinforces them and neglect what opposes them. Changing our beliefs requires a focus on all the facts and not just those that feed the beliefs that are unwanted.

Identify Your Core Beliefs

Beliefs can be formed because of a number of factors. Most teens tend to develop core beliefs through their experiences and the way their caregivers treat them or act around them. For example, teens may develop a core belief about money that is negative when they constantly witness their parents stressed overpaying bills. Parents who constantly warn their children to be careful may instill in their children a core belief that the world is an unsafe place or to look at many things as a threat. Both these examples can cause children to grow into teens and then adults who are anxious.

Additional beliefs may have developed at a young age for good reason but no longer serve you well as you get older. For instance, a child that grows up in an abusive household may develop the core belief that they are powerless or that sticking up for themselves only brings about more suffering; they develop the belief that they are helpless. As the child grows and moves away from this toxic environment, this core belief no longer serves them.

When you are trying to identify your core beliefs, the first place you can turn to is your thoughts. Your thoughts can help you notice themes, and these themes can be the foundation for your core beliefs. Ask yourself some of the following questions to identify your core beliefs.

- What events in your life may contribute to your beliefs?
- What is your family dynamic like?
- What lessons did you learn from an early age?
- How have or do these lessons affect the way you see the world around you, the people you encounter, and the way you view yourself?

Changing Negative Beliefs

For many, our beliefs are formed by simply believing what is told to us. Since at a young age, we are unable to understand whether something is fact or opinion, we simply go along with what we are told. These negative beliefs can result in developing anxiety, phobias, anger issues, and being shy.

- **Negative beliefs and anxiety** - The negative beliefs that are attached to anxiety are often one of the weaknesses. When we strive to be perfect, we can feel a great deal of disappointment with ourselves and from others. We can place too much pressure on ourselves and place a significant amount of importance on meeting other people's expectations. This can lead to thoughts and fear of failure and what others may think of you. This in return triggers an enormous amount of anxiety.

145

- **Negative beliefs and phobias** - Fear makes us behave and thing in highly negative ways. An extreme fear of people. places or things cause use to develop phobias around those factors. Phobias are often an irrational fear. We may have no real reason to be afraid but have strengthened this fear through our thinking and actions so that we feel paralyzed when confronting these phobias.

- **Negative beliefs and anger** - Irrational anger is destructive and enables us to think clearly. This will often result in destructive behavior. Extreme anger can result in chronic stress and can also transform into depression. When we are unable to manage our anger, properly express our anger, or control our impulses when frustrated, we do or say things we regret. Beliefs that form around anger are often a result of trauma or negative experiences that we never took the time to reevaluate or talk through.

- **Negative beliefs and shyness** - Shyness can often develop out of fear. You might formulate the belief that you act awkward in social settings because you heard over and over that you are just shy. In reality, you may have never noticed that your behavior could be taken negatively and instead of trying to change your behavior in social settings, it was justified. You may not be shy at all, but it becomes your default response when you don't talk as much or interact when around others. Simply having this belief could be the whole reason why you don't speak up more.

Negative core beliefs impact our thoughts, feelings, and behaviors, and changing them will take time and persistence. To rid ourselves of these negative beliefs, there has to be a new positive belief that replaces them, and a new way of thinking needs to be implemented to support these new beliefs.

To create new positive beliefs, you will need to learn to anticipate when the negative beliefs arise. There are countless situations in your day that will trigger limiting beliefs to arise, and each situation will cause you to respond and cycle through negative thoughts. Begin to record when these negative beliefs arise and the thoughts that follow.

When you want to change your core beliefs, you must first identify what those beliefs are. Think about all the areas of your life; which areas do you want to see an improvement in? Consider how you might have attempted to improve these areas before. What thoughts surround how you feel about your efforts in improving these areas? What behaviors do you notice when you are confronting these areas of your life? Are there areas of your life you are not happy about or that you don't feel fully connect or committed to? Are there areas of your life that make you feel inadequate, powerless, or held back?

Once you are able to answer these questions, you can begin to log your day. Creating a log can help you identify when your thoughts, behaviors, or emotions are motivated by a negative belief. You can then begin to rephrase the thoughts you have around the belief and transform it into one that is more positive.

Create a log

Situation: *When did the negative occur. Who were you with? What were you doing?*

_____

_____

_____

_____

_____

Belief: *What was the negative belief?*

_____

_____

_____

_____

_____

Negative Thoughts: *What thoughts occurred when you noticed this belief?*

_____

_____

_____

_____

_____

New Positive Belief: *What is a more empowering belief you can have in this situation?*

_____

_____

_____

_____

_____

Realistic thoughts: *What evidence do you have that supports this new positive belief?*

_____

_____

_____

Create a log like this every time you find yourself stuck on a negative belief.

Determination and Commitment

Determination is necessary if you are going to overcome any hardship in life. You will need to determine when things become uncomfortable or when you face challenges that bring on an overwhelming number of negative thoughts and emotions. Without determination, you will never be able to follow through on the commitments you make with yourself or to the goals you want to achieve.

If you want to be able to overcome your fears, anxiety, depression, negative thinking, or destructive behavior, you need to be committed to the process. Completing the exercises in this book is proof of that commitment. Implementing the tips, techniques, and tools outlined in the following pages will take determination. Trying once and not getting the desired result will not allow you to see the changes you want. Utilizing these CBT guides will allow you to fully understand all the potential you possess and will allow you to reach that potential.

Fully understanding how your thoughts, behaviors, and emotions all affect one another will allow you to better determine and commit to the changes you seek. Focusing on each of these areas and being honest with yourself is the most effective way to produce change. Not only will these changes immediately benefit you as you navigate your teenage years, but they will benefit you even more as you move into adulthood.

Exercises

Rethinking Your Thoughts

You can notice your negative core beliefs easily if they tend to be an all-or-nothing phrase. Meaning you have the same belief no matter what situation you are in. When you have these beliefs, there are a number of questions you can ask yourself and steps you can take that will help you reword the negative beliefs. Below, you will find some of the most common negative beliefs as well as exercises you should complete if you have these negative beliefs. Go through each one and feel free to add your own negative beliefs and what you can do to counter them when they arise.

I am worthless.

- Create a list of at least five qualities that make you unique.
    1. _____
    2. _____
    3. _____
    4. _____
    5. _____

- Write three things you did today that helped others.
    1. _____
    2. _____
    3. _____

- Write the names of three people who care about you.
    1. _____
    2. _____

3. _____

- Reevaluate the situation where this belief came about. What triggered this belief?

_____

_____

_____

_____

- Identify one fact about the situation that opposes this belief.

_____

_____

_____

_____

I am always wrong.

- What is one subject in school that you excel in?

_____

_____

_____

_____

- Give three examples where you could have made a poor choice but instead choose to do the right thing.
    1. _____
    2. _____
    3. _____

- Reevaluate the situation where this belief came about. What triggered this belief?

_____

_____

_____

_____

_____

- Identify one fact about the situation that opposes this belief.

_____

_____

_____

_____

_____

I can't do anything right.

- List three times when you felt proud of yourself.
    1. _____
    2. _____
    3. _____

- List three times when you answered a question correctly.
    1. _____
    2. _____
    3. _____

- Give an example of when you made your parents, teachers, or friends proud.

_____

_____

_____

_____

_____

- Reevaluate the situation where this belief came about. What triggered this belief?

_____

_____

_____

_____

_____

- Identify one fact about the situation that opposes this belief.

_____

_____

_____

_____

_____

I am unwanted.

- Reevaluate the situation where this belief came about. What triggered this belief?

_____

_____

_____

- Identify one fact about the situation that opposes this belief.

_____

_____

_____

_____

Nobody likes me.

- List the names of three of your closest friends.
    1. _____
    2. _____
    3. _____

- List all the family members you see regularly.

    1. _____
    2. _____
    3. _____
    4. _____
    5. _____

I am stupid.

- Reevaluate the situation where this belief came about. What triggered this belief?

    _____

    _____

    _____

    _____

    _____

- Identify one fact about the situation that opposes this belief.

    _____

    _____

    _____

    _____

    _____

I always get left out.

- Reevaluate the situation where this belief came about. What triggered this belief?

_____

_____

_____

_____

_____

- Identify one fact about the situation that opposes this belief.

_____

_____

_____

_____

_____

I am no good at anything.

- Reevaluate the situation where this belief came about. What triggered this belief?

_____

_____

_____

_____

- Identify one fact about the situation that opposes this belief.

_____

_____

_____

_____

NEGATIVE BELIEF	NEW BELIEF
I AM WORTHLESS	I AM PROUD OF WHO I AM
I AM ALWAYS WRONG	I AM ALWAYS LEARNING SOMETHING NEW
I CAN'T DO ANYTHING RIGHT	I AM GOOD AT A LOT OF THINGS
I AM UNWANTED	I AM LOVED
NOBODY LIKES ME	I AM SURROUNDED BY PEOPLE WHO LOVE ME
I AM STUPID	I AM ABLE TO LEARN WHAT I DON'T KNOW
I ALWAYS GET LEFT OUT	I AM FUN TO BE AROUND
I AM NOT GOOD AT ANYTHING	I AM CAPABLE OF ANYTHING

Defining the Objective

Now that you have identified the areas of life you want to improve in the previous chapter and understand how your beliefs impact the way you think, feel, and behave, you can create a goal to work toward.

- Identify one area of life you want to improve.

- List the negative beliefs you have toward this area of life.

- Create new positive beliefs that will help you work toward improving this area.

- List three things you can do that will improve this area.

- What would making these changes mean?

AREA YOU WANT TO IMPROVE:	
_____	
_____	
NEGATIVE BELIEF:	
_____	
_____	
NEW BELIEF:	
_____	
_____	
GOAL 1:	
_____	
_____	
WHY IS THIS IMPORTANT TO YOU?	
_____	
_____	
ACTION	1. _____
STEP	2. _____
	3. _____

Chapter 4: Values

Values are the guiding post that will help you become the person you want to become. Values will help you set and achieve goals that will allow you to be successful in life based on what is important to you. Values shape the relationships you have, the activities you participate in, and how you engage in the world around you.

What Are Values?

Values are established by you but can be imposed on you from an early age. Oftentimes, teenagers will adopt the values of their parents or will base their values on their upbringing. Though some may be modified as you get older to better align with who you are, they are often continuous or there is no endpoint. Values are not goals they are linked directly to who you are as a person, what you enjoy, and what matters most to you. When we do not recognize our own true values and only live our life according to the values we have aligned with based on our childhood, we can live an entire life that is not the life we had wanted.

Values can be big and small. They are personal to each person uniquely. For each area of your life, you may have one or many core values. To identify your own unique values, you will need to look at a number of factors.

Identify Your Values

First, how you were raised affects your values. Consider the values you identify with that are because of how you were raised (be respectful to your parents, follow the rules of the house). What values do your parents identify with (being viewed as educated, being viewed as hard-working)? What values are present in the way you live your life or in the way your parents live their lives (you focus on getting good grades because education is important, you remain quiet when adults are around and never voice your opinion)? What values are stressed in your family (you regularly practice a certain religion, there is regular quality time with family such as game nights or vacations)? How were values present to you when you were facing a consequence for your behavior or actions, either as a reward or punishment (you made high honors so you got a new game system, you disagreed with what your parents told you so you got your phone taken away)?

Next, consider the things that you do. Do you play sports, do well in school, play an instrument? Why do you participate in these activities? Is it for enjoyment or to please your parents? What subjects interest you or what topics do you like to talk about with your friends or family? What can you find in this interest that led you to something you value?

Now, consider how the answers to these questions reflect how you were brought up? Are there some values that stick out that do not completely resonate with you? Are there some that you want to strengthen your connection with?

Why Are Values Important in Life?

Your values will help guide you to make the right choices in your life. When you establish your values, you can also come up with new ways to achieve the goals you set. These activities will support your values and feel more rewarding.

Values will allow you to align your behavior and thoughts in a way that helps you succeed. They will help you decide what friends you should keep, what career to pursue, how you want to be viewed by others. and what goals to set. Values are what will motivate you to pursue goals. They are not a goal of themselves but are a standard to how you want to experience the world around you. For a teen, you may not fully understand all the values you may want to adopt or know which are the most important to you. As you get older, new values will come about that will dictate how you live your life. Below, you will find a list of some of the most common early values that you might find important.

Freedom/Independence

For a teen, freedom often reflects how responsible we think we are or how responsible our parents think we are. Every teen strives to have more freedom. They want to stay out later with friends, get a job, and be able to buy things with their own money. They want to feel as though they are capable and that their parents trust them to make good decisions.

Love

Teens need to feel loved and understand that they are capable of loving others. A teen who values receiving love and affection may align their behaviors in a way that allows them to achieve this goal. They may be more respectful, considerate, or caring toward others. However, if they often lack or are unable to appropriately understand what love is or is supposed to look like, they may find themselves valuing having loving relationships but not understand what that is really supposed to be like.

Friendship

What type of relationship do you want to form with your friends? What value would you place on having strong and meaningful friendships? How do you want to be viewed as a friend?

Loyalty

Loyalty is a reflection of trust. Not only do we want to have loyal friends but we want to be viewed as loyal ourselves. Loyalty is related to being able to trust those around you and being able to trust yourself. Loyalty is what will allow you to make commitments to yourself and others and follow through on what you say you are going to do.

Respect

Respect is connected to self-respect. To be able to respect others, we must first learn to respect ourselves in a positive way. Developing respect and self-respect is vital to having a successful relationship with peers, family, and yourself. Being able to see the value *you offer* to others will make it easier for you to see the value *in* others as well. When you treat yourself with respect, it sets a standard for how you want others to treat you as well.

Faith

Faith can mean a number of things to different people. Your faith is often the result of how you are brought up. For many teens, this value is one that is instilled in them from their parents or community. They may value faith but have no real reason as to why this may be important. Additionally, they may be limited in their options to pursue different spiritual paths. Spend some time determining what *you* put faith in.

Family

What types of relationships do you want to have with your parents, siblings, and other family members? How do you want your role in the family to be viewed?

Safety

Feeling safe and secure is a deeply rooted value. From birth, children have a need to feel as though they are safe and protected. When safety is not a concern, it can lead to making poor decisions, hurting others, and being unkind to yourself. Safety as a value requires you to focus on what makes you feel safe, how others make you feel safe, and what makes you feel unsafe.

Success

Success is different for everyone. As a teen, success might simply mean making the varsity team; for others, it could mean being awarded a scholarship at the most prestigious school in the country; and for some teens, success is finding joy and happiness is what they do. In general, though, success is accomplishing the goals you set for yourself through hard work, dedication, and persistence.

Health

For teens, their health may not be a major concern. They may not understand or have ever been taught the importance of maintaining good health. But it is a value you want to seriously consider. Having good health allows you to be more active in your own life. When you are healthy, you not only feel physically strong but mentally strong as well. Adopting health as a value doesn't have to mean never eating cookies and cake or running 6 miles a day. It can simply mean that you take care of the body you have mentally, physically, and emotionally to the best of your ability.

Recognition

Valuing recognition means that you not only want to ensure that others see and acknowledge your accomplishments but that you take the time to do the same for others. Recognition can help us feel good about ourselves and can validate our hard work, but it can also lead to attaching too much importance on how others view you.

Popularity

For many teens, popularity is a high priority on their value list. Being popular often means you are less likely to be bullied, will receive special treatment, and experience a boost your self-esteem. Popularity, however, does not play a vital role once you enter into your adult years. Being popular may be a value while in high school, but developing your own self-worth, self-respect, and self-esteem that will carry on after high school and help you succeed in life may be more important.

Free Time

Teens have a lot on their plate, and a majority of their time is spent in school and completing schoolwork. Add in household responsibilities, extracurricular activities, and a job, and many are left with very little free time. Placing free time as a top value can help teens understand how to balance all the daily demands of life and responsibilities with things they enjoy doing and time to rest and relax.

Gratitude

Gratitude is a powerful and effective way to bring more happiness into your life. From a young age, children and teens who are able to show and be more grateful for what they have tend to be happier and more successful. Gratitude is the act of being thankful and aware of the things you do have. You can be grateful for what you have and still work hard to obtain the things you want but when you do not succeed or get what you wish for, you are less likely to be devastated by the outcomes or length of time it takes to obtain what you are working for.

Happiness

Happiness is connected to a number of areas in your life. Happiness is not just a feeling or emotion but can also be a way of living. Those who value their own happiness and the happiness of others tend to feel as though they belong or are accepted. Happiness is a choice that one makes. Choosing happiness as a core value will help guide you through making tough decisions. It will also remind you to stay true to yourself and can boost your self-worth.

When you know the values you hold, you can better make the necessary adjustments to your thoughts, emotions, and behavior to align with these values. Your values will play a vital role in your success in overcoming obstacles in your life. These values will help guide you in making the best choices and will assure that the choice you make will benefit you.

How Do Our Values Influence Our Choices and Behaviors?

Your personal values will be what can guide you through difficult choices. When you have identified your values, your behaviors will align with what supports those values. How you show up, the relationships you build, and the effort you put into school and work will all reflect on your values. Values can be used to ensure that your behavior or response to challenging situations is how you should be behaving based on who you are and who you want to be.

Moral Dilemmas

Teens are confronted with moral dilemmas frequently through the young adult years. These circumstances are what will help develop and be able to regulate their emotional and behavioral responses in a variety of situations. These moral dilemmas will allow teens to cope and work through social influences. When they have clearly identified their core values, teens are able to more easily work through these uncomfortable moments. When they have not identified their values, teens can suffer from anxiety and depression.

Understanding the Values of Our Life

Values are a way of understanding who you are and who you want to be. When you identify your values, you can use them as a way to stay centered and happy no matter what situations you may be confronted with. Your values can help you understand why you do things the way you do, whether in how you behave, think, or approach certain situations.

Values are not just a guideline for how we behave or act; they can also inspire us to work through problems. Your values will reflect what is most important to you.

When you are clear about what is important to you, then you will be able to make choices and behave in alignment with these values. Teens are faced with a variety of situations where having clear values will help them make the best choice, such as drinking and driving, join their friends when they make fun of the new student, or neglecting homework to play video games. Values can be reviewed and addressed for big and small decisions.

How Values Guide Us

Values guide us by reminding us what is important to us. In each situation, you face you can simply ask what is more important to you. You will make the choice that best aligns with your values. When trying to make a choice between two options, being reminded of the person you are and the person you want to become will make the choice much easier.

Exercise

The Pyramid of Your Values

Choose 5 values and list them in order of importance. You can do this easily by thinking of them on a pyramid. The most important value will go at the top.

When ranking your values, take into consideration the ones you want to be working toward first. The values you rank here will be a reference as you work through your challenging thoughts and behaviors. They will allow you to set specific goals that you can begin working toward achieving using the information throughout this book.

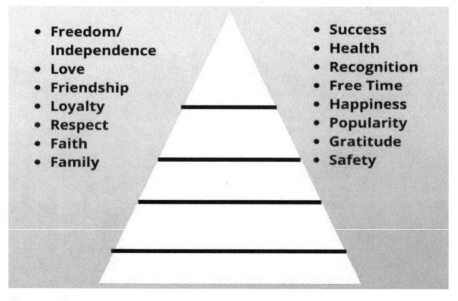

- Freedom/
  Independence
- Love
- Friendship
- Loyalty
- Respect
- Faith
- Family

- Success
- Health
- Recognition
- Free Time
- Happiness
- Popularity
- Gratitude
- Safety

Once you have listed your values, consider what core beliefs you have and what areas of life these values fall into. Are there thoughts, emotions, or behaviors that you exhibit that do not align with these values? List them out.

Chapter 5: Conquer Negative Thinking

Thoughts are meant to come and go. When we get stuck on certain thoughts, we can end up acting out in unfavorable ways. Negative thinking that you allow to consume your day can lead you to make decisions that have severe consequences. Learning how to acknowledge these thoughts, see them as they are, and allow them to flow away from you will allow you to have more control over all areas of your life.

How Do Negative Thoughts Arise?

Thoughts are one of the key components of CBT. We have millions of thoughts throughout the day, and most go unnoticed but have a significant amount of influence on our actions and behaviors without us even realizing it. Some thoughts leave you running in circles, lower your self-esteem, and keep you from remaining in the present moment.

Thoughts can flow through your mind as a simple word, a phrase, or an image. Some of these can be difficult to ignore or move through your thought process and feel as though they are just stuck in your head. This can lead to what is referred to as ruminating. This is excessive worry or focusing on things that can go wrong in the future. These thoughts are often unhelpful and can even be harmful.

Though it may feel as though some of these thoughts are stuck in your mind like superglue, thoughts are just the chatter that takes place in your head. Most of these thoughts have no significant meaning. They are often just a replay of events that have or may occur. Though they feel as though they can consume you, you can learn what chatter you tune into. You can learn to watch your thoughts just as they are, chatter. You can learn to tune out the negative chatter and turn up the positive thoughts.

When you learn to catch the negative thoughts you can learn to decipher the misleading assumptions that are connected to them. Negative thoughts can cause us to make careless mistakes, harm ourselves or others, and can cause problems with family, friends, and at school.

Our thoughts affect our behavior in a number of ways. Do you forgive or retaliate, withdraw or engage, give up or persevere? Your thoughts will either help you alleviate the stress and challenges you face or they can cause you to prolong and find it more difficult to get over some obstacles.

Negative Automatic Thoughts

Negative automatic thoughts are considered a cognitive distortion. These thought patterns are often the result of constantly using "I should" statements. Individuals who suffer from anxiety and depression will have many more negative automatic thoughts. We often feel as though we have no control over negative automatic thoughts. These thoughts are triggered by certain cues and can tear us down. But, these negative thoughts can be used to help build us up, and they can be used to work in our favor to be more successful. When these thoughts tear us down, we suffer from more anxiety.

What Feeds Our Negative Thoughts?

When a negative thought occurs, there tends to be a snowball effect that happens. One negative thought can cause another, then another, and another. The more we are focused on the negative thoughts, the stronger they grow. Our behaviors, emotions, and thoughts all feed into negative thinking patterns. We develop habits that make us feel as though it is perfectly normal to constantly fight off or cycle through negative thoughts. In reality, negative thoughts occur more often once you get into the habit of giving them so much attention.

168

Emotions play an integral role in negative thinking. Many times, we may not understand where our negative thoughts are coming from, but we may notice a change in our body such as feeling more tense or nauseous. These are clear signs that your negative thoughts are occurring because of unrecognized emotions. Once we do recognize the emotion, more negative thoughts form. Emotions, however, can be simply accepted and then let go. Once they run their course, you can shift to more positive feelings. If you focus on the negative thoughts that are occurring at the same time as the emotion, it is more likely that this will prolong the emotional reaction you are having.

When we are out of tune with ourselves and our bodies, this can fuel negative thinking as well. Those who are more self-aware tend to have more positive thoughts. Those who lack understanding in themselves will often find it more difficult to redirect negative thoughts or even spot the negativity before it has spiraled out of control.

How Negative Thinking Affects Our Lives

Our negative thoughts can make us believe in the false assumptions we may form about ourselves, others, and the world around us. Though these thoughts have no truth to them, you can easily jump to a conclusion when a negative thought enters your mind.

Negative thoughts can take us away from the present moment. When a negative thought arises, we automatically tune in, out of habit. Then we get sucked into the negative spiral and miss out on enjoying what we are actually doing. Negative thoughts can also make us want to avoid situations we know will trigger the negativity.

Additionally, negative thoughts can make us more prone to a number of mental health issues such as anxiety and depression. Negative thoughts cause us to go into high alert as they often signal the brain and the body that something is wrong, even if there is no real threat.

169

When confronting problems, negative thoughts make it more difficult for us to find solutions or work through the problem. For teens, negative thinking not only makes it more challenging for them to address their problems, but it makes it more likely for them to make a choice the results in negative consequences.

Negative thoughts affect how we think about ourselves, others, and the world around us. When you have negative thoughts, you may automatically make negative assumptions, and your behaviors will align in this same negative manner. Identifying not only your negative thoughts but your negative thought patterns can help you make major improvements in multiple areas of your life.

Five Negative Thinking Habits

Negative thinking habits can be easier to stop once you are able to identify which patterns they fall into. Below, you will learn about the most common thinking patterns that you may struggle with.

"I Can't" Habit

This negative thought pattern constantly has you focusing on what you are lacking. "I can't" thoughts arise when you face new encounters or difficult situations. When these thoughts occur, they can lead to feeling anxious or sad. You may feel as though you can't make new friends, you can't pass your math test, or that you can't do anything right. The "I can't" negative thought process is most often due to focus on past failures or on beliefs that others have imposed on you.

"All or Nothing" Habit

All-or-nothing thinking is also known as black-or-white thinking. This thinking involves only seeing the extreme results, which can be one way or the other where there is no gray area. This type of thinking is common for those focused on being a perfectionist, or those that always perceiving themselves as a failure when they do not meet their own expectations.

A few examples of this type of thinking could be:

- Thinking you failed a test just because you do not get a 100%.
- Always thinking nothing good ever happens to you just because one thing in your day goes wrong.
- The people around you are either your best friend or your worst enemy.

When you suffer from this type of thinking, you never see the middle ground. To change this type of thinking, you need to catch these extreme "one side or the other" thoughts and counter them with alternative thoughts that are supported by facts.

When you are constantly in the all-or-nothing thought pattern, you may find that you catastrophize things, only see the negatives in the situation, or may blame yourself for problems that have nothing to do with you. When you think in this extreme manner, you quickly lower your self-esteem and begin to take responsibility for issues in other people's lives that you had nothing to with. These thoughts will often arise as a simple negative and quickly spiral out of control, especially when you do not stop to consider all the facts or the lack thereof.

Exercise

Can you think of a time when you had all-or-nothing thoughts? List three of them now.

1. _____
2. _____
3. _____

Now, list three alternative thoughts that oppose these thoughts. These new thoughts should be somewhere along the middle ground of the extreme spectrum.

1. _____
2. _____
3. _____

"I Should, You Should" Habit

When you have the habit of thinking in the "I should, you should" thought pattern, you most likely are applying strict rules to yourself and others. When you have this type of thought pattern, you run into the challenge of not being able to be flexible with others and therefore always feel let down. The "I should, you should" way of thinking often fuels feelings of guilt; you might focus on what you should have done in a certain situation or what someone else should have done.

This thought pattern can also make it more difficult for you to identify or acknowledge that there are things you may not actually know. You might see this thought pattern occur frequently when you need to do a group project, when you are at work, or even when you are just trying to decide where to hang out with your friends.

Getting stuck in the "I should, you should" thought pattern can lead to ruminating over your experiences. You may spend an exuberant amount of time overthinking how you performed on a test, what you said to your crush, or what someone else said to you early in the day. When we get stuck ruminating on the events that occurred, we will feel more anxious, frustrated, disappointed, and stressed.

"It's Not Fair" Habit

The "it's not fair" thinking habit can be a common negative thought pattern for many teens. You may feel as if you were completely deserving of an A or that it is not your fault a certain event occurred. You will blame others for your own failures and never actually analyze the situation to find out what went wrong, so you are unable to make improvements within yourself.

This negative thought pattern does not allow you to grow and be successful. Since you never address what you could have done differently, you never know how to improve. When you get stuck in this pattern, you will often avoid taking chances and never fully apply yourself so that you can live up to your full potential, and this can lead to depression and anxiety.

"Mind Reading" Habit

Those who adopt a mind-reading thought process tends to be 100% certain of what others are thinking with or without facts to support these thoughts. This results in constantly making assumptions about others and always thinking you know what the other person thinks and wants.

Prime examples of mind reading include:

- When someone does not say "Hi" to you, you immediately think they hate you.
- When your friend doesn't respond back quickly after you send them a message, you begin to think they are mad at you and you begin to think of all the reasons they could be mad at you.

When you catch yourself stuck in this mind-reading habit, you need to look at things from the other person's perspective. Look at the situation in which this negative thought arises and consider the facts that are observable from the other person's point of view, not just yours. Once you have filtered through the facts, you need to remind yourself that there is no way for you to know what the other person is thinking, and you have no idea what may have happened before you encountered this person.

Exercise

Think of times when you have gotten stuck in a mind-reading habit and write three examples now.

1. _____
2. _____
3. _____

Now write three new thoughts that will help you remember that unless they have told you, you have no idea if there is proof in these thoughts.

1. _____
2. _____
3. _____

Eliminating Negative Thoughts

You can begin to identify these negative ways of thinking by becoming aware of how these thoughts can affect you. Some cues that you are stuck in a negative thought pattern include:

1. You feel a sudden onset of negative emotions such as anxiety or resentment. When you feel a sudden shift in your emotions, you are most likely dealing with a negative thought.

2. You can't seem to get yourself out of a negative mood. These moods are often fueled by negative thoughts. If you notice that you are irritable during the day for no apparent reason or you feel dread throughout the day, these are clues that you are battling with negative thoughts.

3. Your behavior is not aligning with the goals or values you have identified. When you catch yourself not doing the things you know

175

you should be doing or want to be doing but cannot seem to get yourself to follow through, this is due to negative thoughts.

Negative thoughts can be eliminated using a number of techniques. The first step with any of them is to be able to recognize the negative thoughts and the mind trick you play out when these thoughts occur. To do this, you need to take note of the thoughts that occur in between what happens to you and your response to that event. This is the time period, which is brief, where the negative thoughts will arise and cause you to have behaviors that are unwanted or emotions that are unnecessary. Once you are able to devalue these thoughts, you can create an alternative way of thinking that is based on facts and not just assumptions.

When you get into the habit of being able to identify the negative thinking habits you encounter and write them out, along with an alternative thought, you will begin to realize how inaccurate your thoughts are. After going through this process a few times, you may see these negative thoughts occur less or that you are able to easily debunk them with an alternative thought. Compare your negative thoughts to reality. We feed into our negative thoughts because we do not question how unreasonable or inaccurate they are. When you notice you are having a negative thought, you want to reflect on what has actually occurred without making assumptions. Before you begin to feed into the negative thoughts and reinforce them with behaviors, look for evidence and the supporting facts of the situation.

Hypothesizing

Some thoughts, however, may keep you stuck. No matter how much you believe in the alternative thought you create, the original one continues to show up. It may take a handful of times for you to remind yourself of the alternative thought, and even then, the original thought continues to consume you. When this occurs, there are additional techniques you can use to help move past the negative thinking habit.

One way to counter strong-willed negative thoughts is to test them out. Just as you would test out a hypothesis in a science experiment, you may need to test out your negative thoughts along with the alternative to gather supporting evidence. To accomplish this, you will need to recognize the negative thought, then list the evidence you have both for and against this thought. Once you have your lists, you can look through them and create a new hypothesis or thought that will allow you to move past the negative thought.

Visualization

Allowing thoughts to simply pass through your mind without letting them reel you in is the first step to overcoming your negative thinking. Visualization can assist you in letting your thoughts simply pass through. One way to utilize this technique is to imagine the thoughts that flow through your mind as a cloud. Picture yourself laying under a blue sky in a wide-open field. You see a large, white, cloud begin to drift across the sky. You lay back and watch as it glides across the sky. It may morph into different shapes and take on different forms but, you remain lying on the ground. You watch as it slowly crawls out of sight.

Just as you watch the cloud pass across the sky, you can watch your thoughts pass through your head. As you watched the cloud, you did not get up and begin to drift along under it or with it. You simply let it go in the direction it was going. You can learn to master this skill when it comes to the negative thoughts you approach each day.

Exercises

Focus on Your Strengths

Begin to get into the habit of ending your day by remembering the good that occurred. Each night, write down at least three things that happened in your day that went well. Also, write why these things went well. Completing this exercise each night will support more positive thoughts and can help you shift into having more positive beliefs.

Reframe Your Thoughts

Reframing your thoughts can help you see things from a different perspective, which can have an impact on unwanted behaviors. Exercises to reframe your thoughts include:

1. List the advantages and disadvantages of having the thought and then evaluate the list. You will notice that some of the thoughts are helpful, and others will not align with the goals you have set.

2. List all the possibilities of a situation and then assign them a percentage to how likely it is that one of those other possibilities is actually true as opposed to the way you think about the situation.

Question Your Thoughts

1. What is an alternative outcome that is possible aside from the one you are worried about?

_____

_____

_____

2. Are your emotions clouding your judgment (are your feelings making you feel more strongly about the thought, which is causing you to believe it is true)?

_____

_____

_____

_____

3. What has occurred in a similar situation in the past?

_____

_____

_____

_____

4. How did you get through this situation in the past or what was the outcome?

_____

_____

_____

_____

5. How likely is it that your thoughts are actually true?

_____

_____

_____

_____

6. What is really the worst thing that could happen in this situation?

_____

_____

_____

7. If the worst-case scenario does occur, how would you cope with it?

_____

_____

_____

_____

8. What is another way you can look at this situation?

_____

_____

_____

_____

9. Are you able to predict the future?

_____

_____

_____

_____

Chapter 6: Conquer Anxiety

Worry and anxiety are very similar ways you respond to uncomfortable or new situations. Both worry and anxiety can lead you to act out on irrational thoughts. When you worry, you are constantly thinking about the future. You are unsure of what is about to about or will happen. This is typical when you are concerned about passing a test or if you will find a prom date. This type of worry becomes justified by the thoughts that follow the feelings. Thoughts of having to skip prom, failing a class, having to take summer classes, or miss out on the Friday night game, and a long list of other what ifs, can overwhelm your mind. This leads to an inability to concentrate or remain in the present moment. Worry is a normal characteristic of anxiety. It is normal to worry. It becomes a concern when you are so worried and concerned about the "what ifs" that you are restless.

What Is Anxiety?

Anxiety is the way your body responds to stress. When you are confronted with something you fear or makes you tense, your body and thoughts will mimic the situation. This can result in freezing, trying to get away from what you are encountering, or going into a panic. This anxiety triggers the body's naturally fight or flight response. Anxiety forces us to focus on an imagined threat, which causes feelings of fear or nervousness. These feelings result in behaviors that help us avoid the fear outcome.

You can become physically affected by anxiety. You may feel more aches, pains, headaches, and digestive issues. It can interfere with your sleep, cause you to grind your teeth unintentionally, and can make it difficult to breathe at times. These physical issues can manifest in behavioral issues such as going out of your way to avoid people or places. You may find yourself consumed by a topic or feel the need to spend extra time focusing on finding a solution. You may find yourself so hyper-focused on something that you lose track of time. These behaviors can escalate and turn into more serious issues, like skipping school, intentionally not turning in assignments, no longer participating in extracurricular activities, or not socializing with others altogether.

Though it is natural and even healthy to feel anxious from time to time, when this anxiety becomes overwhelming, lasts for extended periods of time, or comes about with no known triggers, this can turn into a serious anxiety disorder. This extreme type of anxiety can significantly hinder your quality of life and can interfere with your daily routines. Having an anxiety disorder seems like a never-ending battle with your irrational thoughts. Even recognizing your thoughts still doesn't take away the fear and overwhelming sensation. Through deliberate action and clear understanding, you can begin to conquer your anxiety and shift your mindset to one that is more empowering. Anxiety can be used to motivate us and focus on the things that matter most to us.

Where Does Anxiety Come From?

Anxiety can make us feel as though we have no control over ourselves or our surroundings. Though anxiety is a normal and healthy reaction to a situation we are not used to, this can develop into an anxiety disorder that can spiral out of control.

While factors like physical health, hormone balance, and chemicals released by the body impact how you respond to anxiety, a number of other factors play a more significant role. For many, anxiety causes the same reactions to a situation as fear does. The major difference between the two is that people often understand what they are afraid of when they have feelings of fear; with anxiety, it can often be more difficult to understand what the trigger is.

The most common reasons people will feel anxious include:

- Peer or social pressure
- School or work-related pressure
- Family strain
- Health issues
- Substance abuse

When you become anxious you may feel:

- Shaky
- Nauseous
- Stomach discomfort
- Muscle tension
- Headache
- Back pain
- Irregular heartbeat
- Flushed in the face
- Tingling of the hands, arms, or legs

For most individuals, these symptoms of anxiety come and go without much interference. For others, it can be debilitating and cause extreme fears that have no logical explanation. This leads them to avoid what they believe are the triggers for their symptoms. These avoidances can begin small, simply avoiding certain peer circles, and then evolve into more serious issues where an individual may avoid all social settings and isolate themselves.

How Does Anxiety Manifest?

Anxiety disorders are often the result of a number of factors. Life events, genetics, biochemical factors, and personality all have an impact on the development of anxiety disorders. The precise circumstances and triggers are often unidentified until the individual is carefully observed. Only through observation and mindfulness can one begin to understand the true triggers for their anxiety. Anxiety manifests when we imagine there is a

183

threat that may or may not actually occur, and it is fueled through thinking and behaviors.

There are four common features that anxiety will present.

1. There is often an unidentified or unknown debilitating fear. This fear interferes with performing daily tasks and can make it feel impossible to enjoy life.

2. The anxiety the individual feels is often confusing. Because there is no known cause for what is making the individual feel anxious, it can become frustrating and challenging to address or talk about.

3. Even when a logical explanation for the anxiety is identified, there will often be no decrease in symptoms.

4. No matter what type of anxiety disorder you suffer from, understand there is a way to cope, reduce, and even eliminate the anxiety you are suffering from.

Number four is key to remember. Though you may feel trapped by your anxiety now, there are ways you can manage and even eliminate it from your life.

How Does Anxiety Affect Us?

An individual who is able to manage their anxiety can use it to help work through difficult times and avoid dangerous situations. It also helps the individual think more clearly about the situation. When faced with anxiety on a regular basis multiple times throughout the day, it can have the opposite effect. Anxiety that occurs for no reason and causes you to feel panicked or afraid most of the day is a serious concern.

184

Anxiety can have serious effects on your health. The first and most common symptom that an anxiety disorder is present is when you suffer from digestive issues. You may have frequent stomach pains or cramps, lose your appetite daily, and have irregular bowel movements. These issues can worsen over time and weaken the immune system.

Anxiety causes the body to remain in a constant fight or flight mode. When this occurs, the nervous system is working excessively to keep you out of harm's way. While the fight or flight response is necessary when you're actually in a dangerous situation, anxiety causes this state to be on high alert all the time. This can lead to difficulty sleeping, muscle tension, frequent headaches, and constant shifts in your mood.

Being in a constant state of anxiety forces the heart to work overtime as well. When your body is in a constant stressed and anxious state, the heart is pumping more blood and beating faster. This increase in blood pressure can cause excessive strain on the blood vessels.

The most notable way that anxiety can have a negative effect on you is over your quality of life. Living with an anxiety disorder will often limit your ability to socialize, work, focus, and enjoy the things you once loved to do. Anxiety can lead you to feel like a prisoner. Your relationships, both with family and friends, become strained. Many who suffer from anxiety disorders will often avoid meeting new people and will often stop putting effort into the friendships that they have. This only causes the anxiety to worsen and other conditions like depression to develop.

Types of Anxiety

Anxiety is not a one-size-fits-all issue. There are a number of anxiety disorders and anxiety issues that you may be suffering from.

Generalized Anxiety Disorder (GAD)

This type of anxiety causes an excessive amount of worry or fear that continues throughout the day. There is often no specific trigger to bring on the worry or fear, and when it begins, it carries over from one situation to the next.

Phobias

This is a type of anxiety that arises out of fear. Phobias are specific and can revolve around objects, events, or situations. Some of the most common phobias include fear of public speaking, fear of small spaces, fear of wide-open spaces, and fear of spiders.

Shyness

Shyness can transform into a form of social anxiety. While everyone experiences moments of shyness, it can paralyze some teens. Being shy can make it more difficult for teens to interact with their peers and can cause negative thoughts to run rampant through their minds. Shyness can impair your social experiences and cause you to withdraw when confronted with social settings.

For many, being shy is just a part of their personality, and there is nothing wrong with getting a little flushed, shaky, or nervous around others. Feelings of discomfort are a part of healthy social development, and many children will experience these discomforts early on when their trusted caregivers are not by their side. Many children will also experience bouts of shyness when their trusted caregiver is in sight but they are around new or unfamiliar adults. Those who are shy will:

- Be unable to make eye contact when meeting someone new.
- Not speak when they meet someone new.
- Be unwilling to interact with other children they do not know.
- Withdraw and play by themselves.

These behaviors are typical for children when they are placed in unfamiliar situations or when meeting new people. This is a defense mechanism and is completely normal for children still developing their social skills. They will often grow out of these behaviors and will become more comfortable and confident when they face new people and situations.

For some children, getting over these discomforts is more challenging, and shyness can instead strengthen as they grow older instead of diminishing. Other children may have shyness as a fixed component of their personality. These children will often:

- Be struck with anxiety when in social settings.
- Be unable to interact appropriately in social settings.
- Display reserved behaviors in social settings.
- Be overall nervous around others.
- Fear being judged by others.

When shyness is a personality trait, it may not hinder your ability to connect with others. You can still make friends and will be able to excel socially despite the discomfort. These behaviors are concerning when they begin to affect your ability to socialize and disrupt your ability to learn in the classroom. Typical signs of shyness can be an indication of social anxiety disorder. The two may be very similar, but as you will learn, social anxiety disorder hinders teens to a much greater degree than just being shy.

Social Anxiety - As we just discussed, shyness can increase as a child enters their teen years. When this occurs, the teen may be paralyzed when in new or even familiar social settings, resulting in a more serious mental block like social anxiety. Many teens suffer from some form of social anxiety. This type of anxiety is triggered in social settings such as:

- Talking in class.
- Having to give a presentation in class.
- Talking with a group of peers.
- Eating in front of others.
- Attending a party.
- Attending a school function, such as assemblies.
- Having a confrontation with someone else.
- Having attention being directed to them.
- Meeting someone new.

Those with social anxiety are afraid they will do something embarrassing and not only have a negative view of themselves but project the view they have of themselves on how others view them. These fears can keep them from participating in activities that they would find a lot of joy in doing, like playing a sport, joining an after-school club, or participating in group projects.

What makes social anxiety hard to overcome is that the fear we have seems completely logical, and it is hard to discredit because it is based on what we think or how we believe others are viewing us. But since there is no way to know what someone else is actually thinking, that leaves us feeling uneasy and uncertain. Many teens cope with this anxiety by simply avoiding what they know will trigger feelings of discomfort and uneasiness.

How to Eliminate Anxiety

When confronting anxiety, you want to disrupt the negative feedback loop that plays out in your mind. This loop begins when your anxiety is at its lowest effect, but our fear begins to generate additional thoughts that increase the anxiety. When you notice you are beginning to become fearful in a situation, stop and count to ten. This will give you a moment to pause before reacting to your fear. Take a few deep breaths and focus on the facts of the situation. Are you in any real danger? Is anyone else in any real danger? What facts of the situation can you use to contour your negative thoughts revolving around the situation?

Anxiety is not dangerous, and no harm comes from feeling anxious. Though it is uncomfortable, the first thing you can tell yourself when you are feeling anxious is that no harm will come to you. Just because you are feeling an excessive amount of fear does not mean that you are in danger, though that is exactly the way your thoughts and body is responding to this big emotion. Remind yourself that an anxiety disorder is based on unrealistic fears.

Allow yourself to confront what you fear. When you are exposed to the triggers for your anxiety, you begin to face them head-on. When you confront your anxiety through exposure, you begin to train your nervous system not to overreact. You build your confidence and strengthen your ability to confront these fears. By regularly exposing yourself to your fear, you become more aware and understanding that your anxiety cannot harm you.

For Parents

Parents, you can help alleviate some anxiety associated with shyness and social settings by reminding your teen of their positive qualities. This will allow them to recognize these qualities and can be the first step for them to feel more comfortable and confident in social settings.

Another way parents can help their anxious teens in social settings is by helping their children understand that being nervous in social settings is completely normal. By normalizing socialization, your teen will feel less alone. Discuss times when you have been nervous meeting new people either as a teen or even as an adult. Talk to them about how it made you feel nervous and shy and what you said to yourself to help you combat these uncomfortable feelings. When your teen recognizes that what they are feeling is normal and nothing to be afraid of, they can build more confidence when they enter social settings.

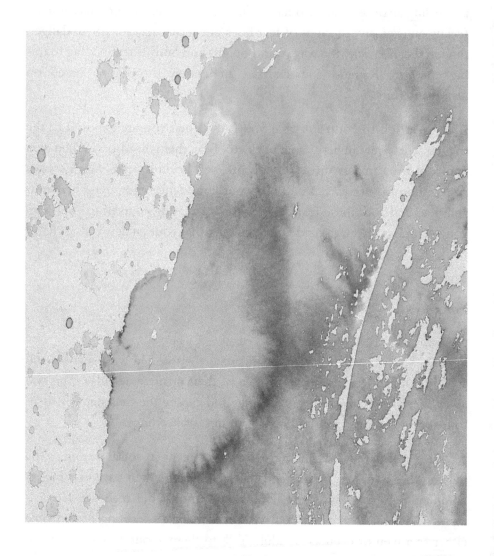

Exercises

Breathing Exercises

Deep breathing is a technique you can use if you are facing a situation that makes you feel anxious and is also great to practice on a daily basis to reduce stress. Deep breathing exercises are easy to do and can help you reduce feelings of anxiety immediately. When you begin to feel fear or anxious, take a deep breath in through your nose for a count of five, then exhale slowly for a count of five through your mouth. Repeat this three times, and you will feel that your body relaxes, your thoughts slow, and you are able to realistically evaluate your situation.

Meditation

Meditation allows you to focus on your thoughts, it can help you train yourself to acknowledge your thoughts and then simply let them go. Meditation for just five minutes a day can help reduce stress, anxiety, and depression.

Begin by sitting in a comfortable position (you can also do this standing). Allow your thoughts to come. When they do come, simply acknowledge them but then let them go. If you find yourself getting stuck on an unpleasant thought or feeling, it can be beneficial to repeat a reassuring phrase to yourself so that you can bring your focus back to the positive, such as "I am safe," or "I am in control," As you get into the habit of meditating, you can add different techniques, like mindfulness.

When you practice mindfulness meditation, you stay in the present moment. Pick something in your environment to focus on; this can be something visual, something you smell, or something you hear. Keep your focus on that object, and when you find your thoughts wandering elsewhere, use that thing to bring you back to the present moment.

Chapter 7: Managing Your Emotions and Moods

Moods and emotions are often used interchangeably, but they have distinct differences. Whereas emotions are experienced frequently and change regularly throughout the day, moods can have a longer-lasting effect. Your mood can affect your daily life, behavior, and thought process.

What Are Moods?

Moods are long-lasting emotional feelings. Moods can feel like phases or stages we go through. They often last a few days at a time but can last for what feels like months with no relief. External circumstances are common triggers for a shift in moods.

It is possible to feel different emotions while you are in a certain mood. You can still feel moments of happiness and joy even if you are in a sad or bad mood. Moods can arise from being overwhelmed by intense emotions that we are unsure of how to manage.

How Our Moods Influence Our Choices and Life

When we are in a certain mood, the way we approach others and the situation will vary. For instance, if you are in an ill or bad mood and you are about to meet someone new, you most likely are not going to be very receptive or optimistic about forming a new friendship with that person. Your behavior will reflect your mood.

Important Moods

There are a number of emotions and moods you will filter through daily. They can come and go, or they can make you feel stuck and out of control. Some of the most common moods you will face and learn to manage include:

- **Fear** - Fear can cause you to become tense and prevent you from living your life the way you want to be living it. Fear can quickly turn into anxiety when we don't stop to recognize or confront what is causing the tension. Extreme fear can transform into anxiety.

- **Anger** - Teens tend to be looked at as just naturally moody. They can snap and become angry in a matter of seconds for what seems to be no apparent reason. Navigating the teenage years leads to experiencing a number of big emotions and social situations that many are ill-equipped to confront. The most natural response for a teen is to lash out in anger. Teens are often looking for more independence but struggle with having to follow their parent's rules to a T. More is expected of them, yet less is offered to them in terms of being allowed more luxuries or freedoms. This anger can quickly turn into long periods of frustration or can result in feelings of hopelessness. As with any emotion, is a natural response, anger can make us act out in unpleasant and unwanted ways. Anger can get the best of you and make you do things you regret. When we respond in the moment of anger, we often act in a way that is opposite of our values.

Anger can be a coping technique you have unintentionally picked up. Instead of dealing and feeling what you are really feeling, you may just default to anger. Often, when you sit and look at your anger, you may uncover that is it actually sadness, fear, or disappointment you are feeling and only covering it up with anger.

- **Sadness** - The teenage years are unfair. Greater expectations are placed on teens that may lead them to feel more disappointed. One of the most common ways for teens to deal with sadness is to withdraw. Sadness can make you feel unmotivated to live up to your potential, socialize, participate in activities, or simply do what you know is expected or that you should be doing. Long periods and frequently feeling sad can lead to feelings of becomes melancholy and depression.

- **Joy** - Joy is a form of happiness. When things are going well, we will feel more joy. There can be spikes in your moments of joy that can leave you in a state of euphoria. Joy can be fueled through gratitude. When we are able to be thankful for what we have and encounter, we are able to find more joy in the things we do.

- **Disgust** - Disgust is a negative feeling in which we often disagree or disprove of what is happening or feel a strong need to avoid what we are encountering. Long periods of disgust or exposure to these unpleasant encounters can transform into hate, annoyance, and loathing. You can feel disgust because of others either because of their actions or words or you can feel disgust for yourself in the way you act, the way you look, or what you have done.

How to Manage Our Moods in Our Favor

To gain better control over your moods, you want to be able to identify what you are feeling. Your thoughts and feelings at the present moment will help you identify the mood you are in. You can do this by simply taking the time to just stop and ask yourself what you are feeling and why. When you notice that your feelings are not suited for the situation you are facing, you can begin to recognize when you need to make adjustments or further evaluate what you are thinking.

Once you are able to state to yourself what you are feeling, you can accept it. Whatever emotion or mood you do uncover, remind yourself that it is normal and OK to feel whatever way you are feeling. What you want to avoid doing is getting stuck on these moods. Instead of allowing your mood to hijack your day, you can acknowledge it and choose to move past what you are feeling.

You can learn to adjust the way you feel to better suit the situation you are facing or in. For instance, you might feel anxious and insecure about competing at a track meet or science fair. But this is not the way you want to feel. You want to feel confident, excited, and alert. You can recognize that the mood you are in is not beneficial, and you can shift it to better suit what you want to accomplish.

Exercises

Mood Awareness

How do the major emotions feel in your body?

_____

_____

_____

_____

What parts of your body are affected when you feel certain emotions?

_____

_____

_____

_____

What urges do you have when you are going through these emotions?

_____

_____

_____

_____

How long do you feel these sensations in your body?

_____

_____

_____

_____

Write

Instead of lashing out in anger at someone or doing something you will most likely regret, grab a notebook and pen and write out everything you are feeling. You can include what someone else has done, how frustrated you are, what you want to yell and scream at them. Whatever it is that you are feeling, stop, and write instead of acting on the mood.

You can write this as a letter addressing the person you feel has wronged you or caused you to feel so intensely or just as a list of thoughts and reactions that you actually are not going to act on.

Once you have gotten everything out of your head at the moment, take note of how you feel. Check in with your emotions and re-evaluate your mood. By doing this, you reduce the risk of acting out on impulse and letting your emotions get the best of you.

Chapter 8: Boost Your Self-Esteem

How you view yourself affects what you pursue in your life. It affects what you will tolerate from others and will allow you to set and keep boundaries in place. There are many ways your self-esteem can impact your behavior and is a direct result of the way you view and think about yourself.

What Is Self-Esteem?

Self-esteem is a positive factor that can give you the confidence to achieve goals, form better relationships, have a positive outlook, and can bring your overall more satisfaction and happiness in all you do. During the teenage years, a young adult's self-esteem will reach phenomenal highs and depressing lows. Because of the many factors that can affect one's self-esteem, it is vital that teens learn to build themselves up and believe in their abilities despite what others may think, say, or how others respond or react to them.

Self-esteem can affect how we relate to others and how we value yourself. Self-esteem can impact physical and mental health. Those who develop low self-esteem are more likely to suffer from anxiety, stress, depression, and have more struggles with substance abuse. Those who have higher self-esteem will place more value on their own strengths and are not constantly seeking approval from others.

When a teen has higher self-esteem, they are able to assert themselves more and are willing and unafraid of trying new things and understand how their actions can have an impact on the world around them. This allows them to

make choices that align their behavior in a way that increases their self-esteem.

What Influences Self-Esteem?

There are a number of factors that can increase or decrease your self-esteem. Self-esteem can be affected by:

- **Friends** - Who we spend the most time with have the most impact on how we view ourselves. Those who have friends that are bad influences will often suffer from lower self-esteem as these friends can cause them to get into more trouble or feed into the negative thoughts they may already hold about themselves.

  Even individuals who aren't considered friends will have a significant impact on self-esteem. Having to deal with bullies and give in to peer pressure can cause a teen to feel bad about themselves.

- **Family life** - Teens who have supportive parents and what is considered a more functional home life will often have higher self-esteem. When the home provides structure and encouragement, a teen will have more positive thoughts and experiences, and this will result in thinking more positively about who they are as a person and what they are capable of. Teens who face unsupportive, overly critical, or absent parents will develop a more negative view on themselves.

- **School and work** - If a teen has unrealistic expectations imposed on them regarding how they perform in school or at work, they can often feel disappointed. When constantly facing this disappointment, their self-esteem can plummet. They can begin to identify and form irrational beliefs based on other people's expectations.

- **How we react to others** - Social interaction also plays a role in self-esteem at a young age. How you behave in front of others can

200

strengthen or decrease how you feel about yourself. If you are always acting a certain way because of the attention it gets from others, you begin to feel as though you are unable to be who you truly are and fear that others may not like you if you are yourself.

How you respond to the way others treat you can impact your self-esteem. If you constantly react in a defensive manner, this is often a result of low self-esteem. If you find that you are unable to stick up for yourself or voice your own opinions, this is also a clear indication of low self-esteem.

- **How we compare ourselves to others** - Constantly comparing yourself to others is the fastest way to decrease self-esteem. For teens, it is almost impossible to avoid comparing yourself with others. You compare your looks, grades, friends, material objects, and everything else with those around you. This will not only decrease your self-esteem, but it can lead to constantly feeling inadequate or that you are lacking. This turns into anxiety and depression.

Additionally, social media, the news, and technology are having a bigger impact on a teen's self-esteem than ever before.

Self-esteem is not a static belief. As we go through different experiences and grow, the way we view ourselves will change and adjust to different circumstances and experiences. Having a healthy balance of knowing and believing in what we are capable of as well as acknowledging the areas we can improve on will allow teens to excel not just in their teen years but throughout their adult years as well.

Low Self-Esteem

Low self-esteem makes us feel uncomfortable with ourselves and therefore makes us feel uncomfortable around others. When a teen suffers from low self-esteem, they are often overwhelmed with self-critical thoughts, and this feeds into making poor decisions. They will often fall into a cycle of making bad choices, which is followed by harsh judgments from parents, teachers, or peers. They process negative thought after negative thought, and this leads them to feel inadequate. Then the cycle repeats continuously, and they never actually learn from the mistakes they made that started the whole process in the first place.

Your thoughts directly affect the way you view yourself, and this affects your behaviors and emotions significantly. When you feel as though you are not as good, smart, capable, or deserving as those around you, you will feel constantly let down, sad, and uneasy when you are with the people you call your friends. When we have low self-esteem, we tend to focus on the negative.

- You only notice your flaws.
- Your self-worth is lower.
- You feel incompetent.
- You feel what makes you unique is a curse.
- You do not take notice of your strengths.
- You feel unworthy of attention or love.
- You are not able to accept compliments.
- You stay in the background.
- You feel more sad or alone.
- You may become aggressive.
- You may be more irritable.

Having low self-esteem can often make you feel as though you are always putting on a show, like you are an imposter and that those around you will figure out that you are not as smart, fun, or enjoyable as you pretend to be. These feelings will affect the relationship you form, and they can lead to you making decisions for other people's approval instead of what you know to be morally right. These feelings also make it more challenging to try new things because you always fear how you will look or what others will think of you. You will turn down or avoid leadership roles or positions and keep you from excelling in the classroom, extracurricular activities, and much more.

For Parents:

You may notice that your teen is suffering from low self-esteem if:

- Your teen talks about being bullied in school.
- Your teen may go out of their way to avoid discussing problems they are having at school.
- Your teen becomes ill more often.
- You notice your teen avoids going out with friends more.
- Your teen begins hanging out with new friends that are a bad influence.
- You notice your teen feeling depressed.
- Your teen ignores what you are saying or ignores punishments imposed because of bad behavior.

Those with low self-esteem are more likely to suffer from mental disorders such as anxiety and depression. For those with lower self-esteem, being able to feel confident and comfortable in front of others is a huge challenge, which is often due to focusing too much on what others think or fearing judgments from those around them.

High Self-Esteem

Those with high self-esteem are often able to look at things realistically. They take responsibility for their successes and failures and are able to bounce back when they encounter disappointment. They don't overreact to situations. If they fail a test, they examine all the factors, and as a result, are able to conclude that they failed because they didn't study thoroughly. They don't think of themselves as not smart or as a failing student. They learn from the mistake of not studying and move forward knowing what to do better next time.

Keep in mind that while you want to have high self-esteem, there is a fine line from crossing over into narcissism. When individuals have too much self-esteem, they may believe that they do not need to improve on anything in their life. They can come off as being self-centered, develop beliefs of entitlement, and never learn from their failures. While high self-esteem is necessary to succeed, not admitting or taking responsibility for things that occur in your life will be a hindrance.

Those who have high self-esteem:

- Understand that confidence is not the same as arrogance.
- Welcome constructive criticism.
- Do not need to please everyone.
- Are not looking for approval.
- Can confront conflict in a healthy manner.
- Set boundaries in their life.
- Can express their needs and opinions in an effective way.
- Are assertive but not pushy.
- Do not strive for perfectionism.
- Can overcome setbacks.
- Can learn from their failures.
- Never feel as though they are inferior to others.
- Are comfortable with who they are.

How We Evaluate Ourselves

If we constantly feel as though we are not equal to or as good as those we surround ourselves with, this will often affect the effort we put into studying, making the right choices, and simply trying out for the things we would truly enjoy participating in a sport or scholarship. Your behaviors will align with the way you think about yourself and what you feel you are capable of.

If you are highly critical of yourself, you may never give yourself the credit you deserve or need to succeed in life. Unfortunately, most of the time we evaluate ourselves, it is in comparison to how others perform against us. Some of these comparisons are based on physical features; others are internal comparisons. When we focus our attention on external comparisons such as worrying about what others think, then we have an increase in self-worth instability. These instabilities increase the risk of depression and unwelcome behaviors. If we learn to make internal comparisons and learn to improve ourselves based on our own accomplishments and abilities, there is less instability, and self-esteem is easier to increase.

Other People's View and the Effect on Our Self-Esteem

When teens are faced with constant disapproval from others, such as their parents, teachers, or peers, they will often develop low self-esteem. But those who already have higher self-esteem are able to accept this disapproval and use it to improve themselves. They do not get caught up on other people's reactions and they do not put all their value or self-worth in the opinions or approval of others.

Social Comparison

Social comparison is the process in which we evaluate ourselves and accomplished against those around us. This type of comparison can affect our social and personal worth. Social media has made it easier than ever to observe and formulate assumptions based on what we see others sharing with the world. Many teens turn to social media to updates and posts from their peers, which can result in a constant state of comparing themselves to others.

Social comparison can be used as a way to acknowledge areas or things you want to improve in yourself; they can be used to motivate you to make improvements, and they can help you develop a more healthy or positive self-image. Unfortunately, social comparison often causes a teen to only focus on their flaws or bring about negative thoughts over never being able to reach the level another peer may be at.

Self-Observation Process

Self-observation is a process in which you focus on yourself in a non-judgmental way. People able to look inside yourself and notice your thoughts, emotions, and behaviors can help you increase your own self-esteem. Self-observation is a way for you to reflect on what makes you unique. It is a way to identify where negative thoughts, beliefs, and behaviors are affecting the way you view yourself or how you want to view yourself. This process allows you to debunk the negative identity that has been formed through social comparison and other feelings of inadequacy.

Cognitive Inferences

Cognitive inferences are what occurs when we form ideas about ourselves with no real evidence to back up these ideas. Also referred to as arbitrary interpretation or arbitrary inferences, we interpret a situation or experience and come to a conclusion about ourselves without considering all the evidence. Focusing on what other people think of us without actually having any clue as to what they are thinking is the most common way we form these types of inferences. We may automatically think that no one likes us or that everyone thinks we are a loser, but in reality, we have no way of knowing what others are thinking. When we form ideas without evidence, we tend to have lower self-esteem.

Selective Abstractions

Selective abstractions are the result of magnifying small negative details that we then use as a foundation to represent who we are. When we evaluate ourselves in this manner, we ignore any positive feedback or positive reinforcements; we only focus on the negative details. These small negative details are then exaggerated. and the way we view ourselves can be completely altered. Selective abstraction causes us to narrow in on negative feedback or reactions from others, and this reaction fuels all the negativity we might feel about ourselves. Even if there is evidence that supports the opposite thoughts, we dismiss the positive evidence. When we evaluate ourselves through selective abstractions, we immediately feel negative about ourselves.

How to Increase Low Self-Esteem

When you are able to identify areas in your life that bring on negative or unwanted thoughts, you can begin to change your through pattern, and in turn, change your behavior so that you can take a chance on more opportunities. By doing this, you will see the way you view yourself changes.

When it comes to increasing self-esteem, the best place to begin is to identify what is causing the low self-esteem to begin with. Oftentimes, negative self-talk and feelings of inadequacy are the root cause of low self-esteem.

One way you can begin to work through this negative self-talk and inadequacy is to recognize that these arise because of how we think others perceive us, not because of who we really are. Work to change those negatives into more positive and affirming statements.

Your self-esteem will begin to improve when you are able to feel more confident in your abilities, talk to your self more positively, and are able to take responsibility for your own actions.

For Parents:

Remember that the way a teen speaks to themselves is often a mirror of how they are being spoken to. If you ridicule your teen because they forgot to do a chore you asked them to do and back up these statements with negative views of them, such as them being lazy or inconsiderate, this only reinforces their low self-esteem.

1. Problem Solving

Problem-solving is a skill teens will greatly benefit from developing earlier on. Since in their adult lives they will be faced with having to make a number of hard decisions and find solutions for their problems on their own this is something that needs to be practiced. Teens that are allowed to work through the decision making progress, test out a solution, and evaluate the results will learn how to effectively solve the many challenges they will be faced with more confidence.

When teens learn to solve problems on their own their self-esteem naturally increases. This is because they learn to feel empowered by the choices they make, even if the results are not what they had hoped for.

2. Self-Talk

Positive self-talk is vital for high self-esteem. Adopting a more positive inner dialog can be challenging for teens as they are often confronted with harsh words from bullies, the media, and others. Being too critical can lead to limiting beliefs of feeling as though you will never accomplish anything, feeling as though you will never be good enough, and can result in teens becoming too eager and focused on being perfect or too discouraged to even try.

Improved self-talk is not something that will easily change overnight. Once you begin to recognize the negative self-talk, you can start to reword what you say so that the dialog that takes place in your head is one that encourages you to improve where you need to improve and to not get stuck on not accomplishing things the way you had anticipated them being done.

3. Self-Control

How we behave in social settings has a lot to do with our self-control. Some teens are unaware of how to take control of their behaviors, and for other teens, anxiety clouds their ability to control themselves the way they know they should or would like to.

Practicing different social situations and modeling self-control behaving is an effective way for teens to learn and improve on their own self-control. The goal is to help your teen become more comfortable in social situations and more confident in their ability to respond in an appropriate way.

For Parents:

Here are some ways you can help boost your teens self-esteem:

- Praise them for their accomplishments, no matter how small.
- Give them credit when they are making an effort, even if the task they complete is not up to your own standards of how it should be done.
- Turn mistakes into an opportunity for them to learn.
- Point out negative self-talk and how they can reframe these to more empowering thoughts.
- Try new things with your teen.
- Allow them to make their own choices and have their own opinions without telling them they are wrong.
- Volunteer with your teen or encourage them to give back to others.

When giving praise, be specific about their accomplishments. Do not fall back on generic praise.

Self-Actualization

Once basic needs are met, like food, shelter, and cleaner air, individuals move on to acquire more fulfilling needs, such as feeling love, increasing self-worth, finding a place they belong, and feeling safe in their environment and with those around them. Self-actualization is the process we go through when we want to add more meaning to our lives through personal and social objectives. We meet these objectives through our creativity, intellectual expansion, and social progress.

Chapter 9: New Thoughts

You learned earlier how to identify your negative thoughts patterns. You learned how your beliefs and values can have an impact and also be affected by your thoughts. Changing the way you think is no easy task. Negative thoughts will creep into your mind and ruin your day if you are not aware of when they occur or how to combat them.

While identifying your thought patterns is the first step, transforming them to empower you will take practice. There are many ways you can shift your thinking. There are effective ways you can reinforce positive thoughts and behaviors that you can adopt to keep your thoughts and actions in line with who you are and who you want to become. Refer back to what your values are. Your values can help you keep your thoughts aligned with what matters most to you.

Exercises

Affirmations

Create your own empowering "I am" statements. Make them personal and specific to the goals you want to achieve. Some examples:

- *I am loved.*
- *I am a great friend.*
- *I am in control of my thoughts.*
- *I am working hard to improve my grades.*
- *I respect my parents, and they trust me to make the right choices.*

Once you have your affirmations in writing, repeat them at least three times a day. Stand in front of a mirror and believe fully in what you are saying to yourself. Do this every day and notice how your behavior begins to change.

When you notice negative thoughts bombarding your mind, repeat these affirmations to stop the cycle and redirect the direction your thoughts go. Notice how your confidence increases, how you approach others differently, and how you treat yourself. Every week, take some time to look over these affirmations and create news ones when necessary. The most important component in writing these affirmations is that you constantly repeat them to yourself. Your negative thought patterns will be disrupted, and your brain will begin to change the way it processes your experience and allow you to have more positive views on what you face and a more positive view on yourself. The more you practice positive self-talk, the more your thoughts will change.

Write your affirmations now.

Create a Let It Go Phrase

Negative thoughts will come and go throughout your day. There is no way to completely eliminate them, but there are ways you can disrupt your typical thought pattern and stop the negative thoughts in their tracks. Instead of giving extra attention and energy to your negative thoughts, have a go-to phrase that allows you to acknowledge then but then simply let them go. This works well when you notice thought that involves a limited or negative belief.

For example:

You notice the negative belief of "I am not good at anything" creep up on you.

You can address this thought by simply stating "Oh, hey that's just nonsense" or "Wow, I can't believe I used to believe that" or "But there are so many things I haven't even tried yet; this cannot be true".

You are adding a bit of humor but also making it known that this thought has no evidence to back it up.

Think of some of the common negative thoughts or beliefs you notice occur regularly. Now, think of a phrase you can say to yourself that will oppose this thought and allow you to see the nonsense of the statement.

You can write it out like this.

Negative thought/belief:

_____

_____

_____

_____

_____

Counter phrase:

_____

_____

_____

_____

_____

Shift to a Growth Mindset

One of the easiest things you can start implementing now to shift your fixed mindset to a growth mindset is to add the word "yet" at the end of those limiting phrases.

- "I'm not good at playing the drums, yet".

- "I'm not fast enough to play football, yet."
- "I am not good with grammar, yet."

Adding "yet" to the end of these phrases immediately begins to shift your fixed mindset to a growth mindset. When you find yourself focused on what you can't do now, add "yet" to what you say to yourself.

Chapter 10: New Behaviors

Behaviors become habitual the more we act on them. Our behaviors are our reaction to internal or external stimuli. How we perceive ourselves, our values, beliefs, and mindset can influence our behaviors and vice versa. When we notice an inconsistency in our behaviors and what we want to be, we can address and change so that everything aligns correctly. Social and peer pressure are the two most common factors that cause our behaviors to act out of line with who we want to be.

Recognize the Behaviors You Want to Change

Some behaviors will not necessarily fall into the category of aligning with your values, but they can be destructive or unhelpful. These behaviors, such as impulsively texting, yelling, or not doing homework, are behaviors you may simply want to decrease or stop. To rid yourself of these behaviors, you have to first be able to notice them as they occur in your daily life. You will want to track these behaviors for two to three days and list the times they occur, the places they occur, and who you are with. The point of tracking isn't to stop yourself at this point from the behavior; instead, you want to know when they are most likely to occur so that you can come up with an alternative behavior to do.

This is challenging as most children are not told what to do; they are only told what not to do from an early age: "Stop running", "don't touch," "no hitting." While this reinforces that you are not supposed to do something, this doesn't direct you to what you are actually supposed to do. Instead, instructions such as "Walk "or "slow down," "keep your hands to your side," "nice hands" are more helpful. While you can identify what you may not want to be doing, the only way you can stop the behavior is if you know what you want to replace the behavior with.

Exercise;

- List three behaviors you would like to decrease or stop.
    1. _____
    2. _____
    3. _____

- Track when these behaviors occur for two to three days.
    1. _____
    2. _____
    3. _____

- List two replacement behaviors for each instance you notice they occur. You can repeat the replacement behavior as many times for different situations as you are able to.

_____

_____

_____

_____

If listing two replacement behaviors is a challenge, then at least come up with two replacement behaviors for each behavior you want to change and use this as a starting point for coming up with more replacement behaviors that can be beneficial in different settings.

Behaviors That Are Beneficial But You Avoid

There may be behaviors you want to adopt but your fear or anxiety holds you back from attempting them. Since you have gone through some of the steps and exercises in conquering your anxiety, you may find that you have more confidence in trying to incorporate more beneficial behaviors. To overcome and adopt new behaviors you avoid out of fear, take steps to gradually become more comfortable in the situations that involve this behavior.

For example:

If you want to participate more in class but have avoided doing so because you fear public speaking, you may begin by simply talking to your teacher or participating in small group discussions more. Over time, you may raise your hand once a week to answer a question, then move up to once a day.

If you fear giving a presentation in class, you might begin by again discussing the presentation with other classmates. Then, you might practice giving the presentation when you are alone, then in front of your family, then friends. The more you practice, the more comfortable and confident you will be in the situation. By practicing, you also allow yourself to stop the negative thoughts you have associated with the behavior you have been avoiding.

Exercise:

- List the behaviors that you want to begin to incorporate into your life that you have been avoiding up until now out of fear or anxiety.

  _____

  _____

  _____

  _____

- List how these behaviors can be beneficial for you in the long-term.

  _____

  _____

  _____

  _____

Positive Reinforcement

Positive reinforcement is essential when it comes to adopting new behaviors. We are more likely to continue to do something when we are getting something out of it, whether it is because the reward aligns with our values, thoughts, or personal preferences. Think about all the behaviors you exhibit throughout the day.

- Helping your friends
- Dong chores
- Finishing your homework
- Being on time for work

Now consider the reasons why you do these things; what do you get out of them?

- Being considered a good friend
- Gaining praise or more independence from your parents
- Getting good grades
- Being viewed as a good employee

There are many behaviors throughout the day you seemingly do by default, but you actually do them because there is some kind of a reward in it for you. When you are trying to change behaviors or begin new ones, one of the first things you can use as motivation is having a simple reward system in place. You want to create a list of positive reinforcements that will help keep you moving in the right direction.

- Buying a new pair of shoes
- Buying a new game
- Watching a new TV series
- Getting your hair done

The reward has to be something that will motivate you and that you won't be able to access until you have successfully adopted the new behaviors.

Exercise:

List the ways you can reward yourself.

_____

_____

_____

_____

_____

Accountability

It is easier for us to follow through on what we promise to others than it is to follow through on what we promise ourselves. When you enlist a close family member or friend to keep you accountable, there is a higher chance that you will be successful simply because you don't want to let the other person down. It is also to have someone in on your goals that you can celebrate your victories with.

Exercise:

List some individuals you can go to for accountability.

_____

_____

_____

_____

_____

Chapter 11: Creating New Objectives?

Setting goals or objectives will help assist you in building confidence and change your negative thinking patterns. Once you have achieved one goal, creating another can be easily done and accomplished. Look back on the previous chapters and take into consideration:

1. The areas of your life you want to see the most progress in.
2. The core beliefs you want to change.
3. The values that are important to you.
4. The negative thought patterns that may create obstacles.

Looking over each of these areas will help you formulate new objectives and create a plan for accomplishing your goals.

Steps for Creating New Objectives

1. Refer back to your value pyramid.
2. Start with the most important value.
3. Come up with a goal that supports this value.
4. What steps do you need to take to achieve this goal?
5. What is the first step you are going to take?

Keep in mind:

1. What are some barriers or obstacles that you may face as you work through each step? (These barriers can also be the negative thoughts that might arise as you progress toward your goal.)
2. What are some solutions that will help you overcome these obstacles?

Why Set New Objectives?

Goals allow you to have a clear vision of where we are going and what we are working toward. When you set effective goals, you can more easily navigate the road before you and set yourself up for success despite the obstacles you may encounter. The goals you set will allow you to determine if the steps you are taking are actually helpful and moving you to where you want to be.

When thinking of your goals, ensure that they are specific, achievable, important, and realistic.

Creating an Action Plan

To set a goal, think about the following questions:

1. What is the first value you want to commit to working toward?

    _____

    _____

    _____

    _____

2. What goals align with this value?

    _____

    _____

    _____

    _____

3. What behaviors do you want to change, stop, or incorporate that align with the value?

_____

_____

_____

_____

4. What specific goal do you want to reach that will help you with these new behaviors?

_____

_____

_____

_____

These goals should be short-term and easy to accomplish. For example, if you want to start exercising, your goal could be to exercise two times that week.

Working in weekly increments will make it easier for you to track your progress and even easier to achieve.

Write out your specific goals for this upcoming week now.

Now, let's put everything together so you can create a plan that is easy to follow.

Date: __/__/____

Goal:

_____

_____

_____

Times and days you plan to work on this goal:

_____

_____

_____

Write the name of those who are keeping you accountable:

_____

_____

_____

Write your positive reinforcement or the reward you will treat yourself with once this goal has been accomplished for the week.

_____

_____

_____

You will do the same plan for the next week, only this time you will review your progress from the previous week. What goals did you struggle with that you will need to come up with a solution for (what barriers or obstacles did you run into while you were trying to accomplish this goal)?

Are there any goals that you swap out for the next-step goals (if one of your goals was to find a job, and the first step was to do a job search, the next step may be getting applications or setting up an interview)?

Were your rewards appealing enough?

Are there some behaviors you can increase the times you do them in the week (instead of working out two days a week, work out three)?

Conclusion

Being a teenager is not easy. Handling big emotions, negative thoughts, and out-of-control behaviors are not easy. As a teenager, you might be trying your best to act the way you are expected, to get the grades you are expected to, and participate in other activities that you expected to participate in. There are a lot of expectations.

It is no wonder that many teens suffer from anxiety, depression, and other disorders that leave them feeling helpless. It is also no surprise that these feelings of helplessness result in behaviors that make them feel in control even though they are not the best behaviors. And, it is also no surprise that these feelings and behaviors are what they will carry on in their adult life.

Your teen years will only last a few years, but what occurs during these years will stay with you for the rest of your life. Adopting a more positive outlook on yourself, those around you, and the world around you can result in great success once you reach adulthood. Cognitive Behavioral Therapy is one way that you can begin to stop the limiting beliefs and views you have on yourself. This book offers you an introduction to the steps you can take to have more control over your emotions, thoughts, and behaviors.

Continue to utilize the tips, techniques, and tools described in the chapters when you trying to make a big decision or improve grades, when you are trying to strengthen your relationships and increase your confidence.

References

Bialasiewicz, K. (2017, December 17). Moods and Emotions: How to Tell the Difference and Make Changes. Retrieved from http://timhillpsychotherapy.com/moods-vs-emotions/.

Chansard, T., & Tikkou, F. (2019). Conquer anxiety workbook for teens: find peace from worry, panic, fear, and phobias. Althea Press.

Gavin, M. L. (Ed.). (n.d.). Choosing Your Mood (for Teens) - Nemours KidsHealth. Retrieved from https://kidshealth.org/en/teens/choose-mood.html.

Sussex Publishers. (n.d.). How Do You Evaluate Your Self-Worth? Retrieved from https://www.psychologytoday.com/us/blog/emotional-nourishment/201804/how-do-you-evaluate-your-self-worth.

History of Cognitive Behavior Therapy - CBT: Beck Institute. (n.d.). Retrieved from https://beckinstitute.org/about-beck/team/our-history/history-of-cognitive-therapy/.

Hutt, R. L. (2019). Feeling better: Cbt workbook for teens: essential skills and activities to help you manage moods, boost self-esteem, and conquer anxiety. Althea Press.

JOSEFOWITZ, N. I. N. A. (2020). Cbt Made Simple: a clinician's guide to practicing cognitive behavioral therapy.

NEW HARBINGER PUB. Sussex Publishers. (n.d.). Personal Growth: Your Values, Your Life. Retrieved from https://www.psychologytoday.com/us/blog/the-power-prime/201205/personal-growth-your-values-your-life.

Recovery Ways. (2018, November 16). 7 Ways Anxiety can Affect Your Life. Retrieved from https://www.recoveryways.com/rehab-blog/7-ways-anxiety-can-affect-your-life/.

Sussex Publishers. (n.d.). Self-Esteem. Retrieved from https://www.psychologytoday.com/us/basics/self-esteem.

Star, K. (2019, November 20). Self-Defeating Thoughts and Beliefs. Retrieved from https://www.verywellmind.com/change-your-self-defeating-beliefs-2584239.

Values Clarification: How Reflection On Core Values Is Used In CBT. (2019, November 20). Retrieved from https://positivepsychology.com/values-clarification/.

CPSIA information can be obtained
at www.ICGtesting.com
Printed in the USA
BVHW092338141121
621672BV00009B/258